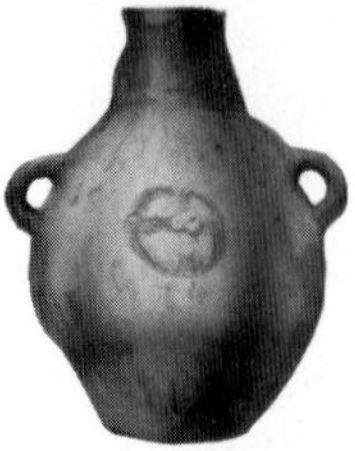

Marhaba lil-Maghreb

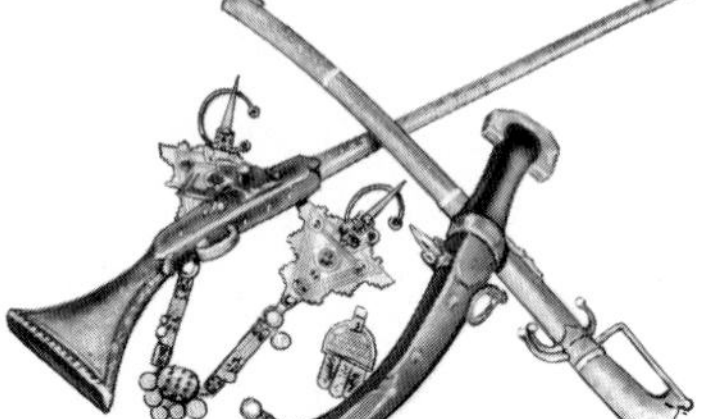

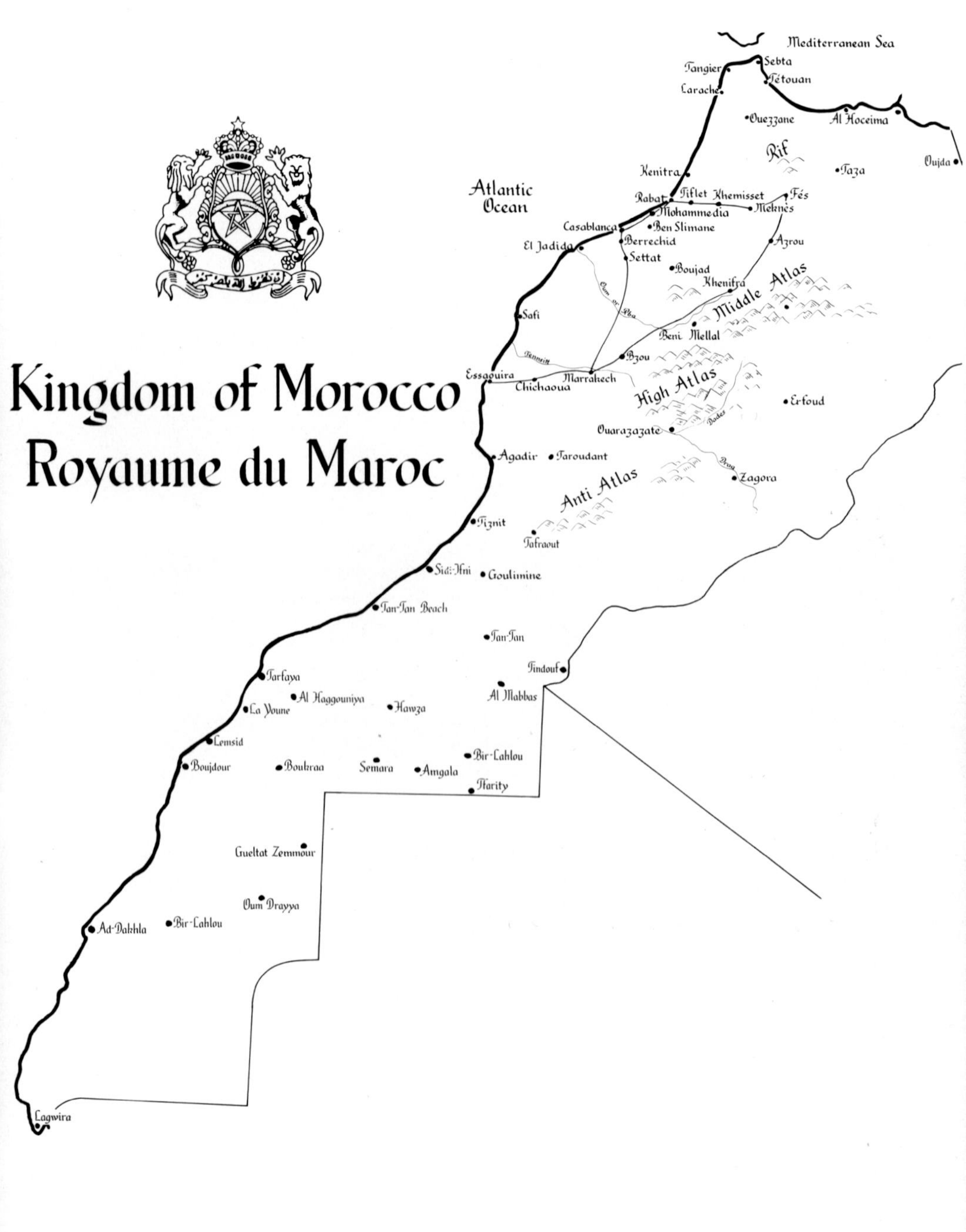

Kingdom of Morocco
Royaume du Maroc
Mediterranean Sea
Tangier
Sebta
Larache
Tétouan
Ouezzane
Al Hoceima
Rif
Oujda
Kenitra
Taza
Atlantic Ocean
Rabat
Tiflet
Khemisset
Fés
Mohammedia
Meknès
Casablanca
Ben Slimane
Berrechid
Azrou
El Jadida
Settat
Boujad
Khenifra
Middle Atlas
Safi
Beni Mellal
Bzou
Essaouira
Chichaoua
Marrakech
High Atlas
Erfoud
Ouarazazate
Agadir
Taroudant
Zagora
Anti Atlas
Tiznit
Tafraout
Sidi Ifni
Goulimine
Tan-Tan Beach
Tan-Tan
Tindouf
Tarfaya
Al Haggouniya
Hawza
Al Mabbas
La Youne
Lemsid
Bir-Lahlou
Boujdour
Boukraa
Semara
Amgala
Harity
Gueltat Zemmour
Oum Drayya
Ad-Dakhla
Bir-Lahlou
Lagwira

Published in the United States by Scenic Publications.
Distributed through the American Museum of Moroccan Art.

 Publié aux Etats-Unis par Scenic Publications. Distribué par le Musée américain d'Art marocain.

Library of Congress Cataloging-in-Publication Data

Taylor, Alf, 1943-.

A Treasure Hunter's Guide to Morocco : a common sense approach to sightseeing, shopping, and etiquette in the land known as Maghreb Al-Aqsa, Islam's Far West / by Alf Taylor ; edited by Ruth Rotert = *Guide du Maroc pour les chasseurs de trésors : une approche pleine de bon sens au tourisme, aux achats et à l' étiquette dans le pays nommé Maghreb Al-Aqsa, l'Extrême Occident de l'Islam / par Alf Taylor ; edité par Ruth Rotert.*

p. cm.

ISBN 0-9628915-0-9

1. Morocco—Description and travel—1981—Guide books. 2. Shopping—Morocco—Guide books. I. Rotert, Ruth. II. Title. III. Title: *Guide du Maroc pour les chasseurs de trésors.*

DT304.T38 1991
916.404'5—dc20 91-9394
CIP

A Treasure Hunter's Guide to Morocco

by Alf Taylor

A common sense approach to sightseeing, shopping and etiquette in the land known as Maghreb Al-Aqsa: Islam's Far West

Edited by Ruth Rotert

Published by Scenic Publications

Distributed by the American Museum of Moroccan Art

Guide du Maroc pour les chasseurs de trésors

par Alf Taylor

Une approche pleine de bon sens au tourisme, aux achats et à l'étiquette dans le pays nommé Maghreb Al-Aqsa: l'Extrême Occident de l'Islam

Edité par Ruth Rotert

Publié par Scenic Publications

Distribué par le Musée américain d'Art marocain

Table of Contents

Table des matières

Photo: Hahn

Potter. Ensemble Artisanal, Rabat.
Potier. Ensemble Artisanal, Rabat.

Dedication

This book is dedicated to the magnificent artisans of Morocco. They use the wood, fabrics, plants, metals and stones available to them to create these wondrous treasures.

This book is also dedicated to the merchants of the souks and marketplaces of Morocco. Without their vigorous assistance we might all go home empty-handed.

And finally, "Treasures" is dedicated to Judi, who told me amicably to "write the book, or stop talking about it!" and then helped me so much to complete it.

Alf Taylor

Dédicace

Ce livre est dédié aux magnifiques artisans du Maroc. Ils utilisent les bois, tissus, plantes, métaux et pierres à leur disposition pour créer ces merveilleux trésors.

Ce livre est aussi dédié aux marchands des souks et des marchés du Maroc. Sans leur assistance vigoureuse nous risquerions tous de rentrer chez nous les mains vides.

Et finalement, ce livre de "trésors" est dédié à Judi, qui m'a dit amicalement "écris le livre, ou bien n'en parle plus!" et qui m'a ensuite tellement aidé à le compléter.

Alf Taylor

Photo: Sisk

Water jug: Blue pottery with brass trim. Fez. Harry and Madelyn McLear collection.
Cruche à eau: céramique bleue à garnitures de laiton. Fès. Collection de Harry et Madelyn McLear.

Embassy of the United States of America

Seeing is believing and A *Treasure Hunter's Guide to Morocco*, with its many beautiful pictures, will convince the reader that the real treasure is Morocco—its warm and friendly people, snow-capped mountains, hundreds of miles of scenic coastline, Imperial cities, and fields of wildflowers. Morocco has long been recognized as one of the most popular developing countries for tourism. Moreover, Morocco has made enormous progress since independence, but throughout this transition, Morocco has remained faithful to the deep roots of its traditions and history.

In recent years Morocco has begun a renaissance in artisanal skills. With a love of Morocco and a keen understanding of the art, antiques, and handicrafts of Morocco, Alf and Judi Taylor have embarked on a journey in their book which will take readers to a unique land and share with them the authors' intimate knowledge and appreciation of Morocco. In learning about Morocco, the reader will find a people in harmony with the land and proud of their work.

I have had the pleasure of traveling to distant parts of Morocco and into numerous medinas and souks with the Taylors, benefitting along the way from their insights and years of experience. In A *Treasure Hunter's Guide to Morocco*, Mr. Taylor, a gifted storyteller and leading authority on Moroccan handicrafts, gives a real feel for Morocco which is rare among travel books. After "Treasure's," readers will be well prepared to explore this fascinating country which is only six hours across the Atlantic and nine miles from Europe. It is, however, a lifetime away from what most have known before.

Michael Ussery
U.S. Ambassador
to Morocco

Embassy of the United States of America

Voir, c'est croire, et le Guide du Maroc pour les chasseurs de trésors, *avec ses nombreuses belles images, convaincra ses lecteurs que le vrai trésor, c'est le Maroc—ses peuples amicaux et chaleureux, ses montagnes aux sommets recouverts de neige, ses centaines de kilomètres de littoraux aux vues éblouissantes, ses villes impériales et ses champs de fleurs sauvages. On reconnait depuis longtemps que le Maroc est un des pays les plus populaires pour le développement du tourisme. De plus, le Maroc a fait d'énormes progrès depuis son indépendance, mais durant cette transition, ce pays est resté fidèle aux racines profondes de ses traditions et de son histoire.*

Pendant les dernières quelques années, le Maroc a connu une renaissance artisanale. Avec un grand amour pour le Maroc et une grande sensibilité envers ses arts, antiquités et produits artisanaux, Alf et Judi Taylor, par ce livre, emmèneront les lecteurs dans un voyage à un pays unique, et partageront avec eux leurs connaissances et appréciation intimes du Maroc. En apprenant davantage au sujet du Maroc, les lecteurs découvriront un peuple vivant en harmonie avec la terre et fier de ses oeuvres.

J'ai eu le grand plaisir de voyager jusqu'aux coins les plus reculés du Maroc et de visiter divers médines et souks avec les Taylors, en profitant de leurs pénétrations et de leurs années d'expérience au cours de ces voyages. Dans le Guide du Maroc pour les chasseurs de trésors, *M. Taylor, un conteur doué et une autorité marquante des produits artisanaux marocains, nous transmet une sensation réelle du Maroc qu'on ne trouve que rarement dans les livres de voyage. Ce livre va bien préparer les lecteurs pour l'exploration de ce pays fascinant qui n'est qu'à six heures de voyage à travers l'Atlantique et à quatorze kilomètres de l'Europe, mais qui se trouve, néanmoins, dans un monde tout différent de celui que la plupart des gens connaissent jusqu'à présent.*

Michael Ussery
Ambassadeur des Etats-Unis
au Maroc

To the Emperor of Morocco.

Great and magnanimous Friend,

Since the date of the letter, which the late Congress, by their President, addressed to your Imperial Majesty, the United States of America, have thought proper to change their Government, and to institute a new one, agreeable to the Constitution, of which I have the honor of herewith inclosing a Copy. The time necessarily employed in this arduous task, and the derangements occasioned by so great, though peaceable a Revolution, will apologize, and account for your Majesty's not having received those regular advices, and marks of attention from the United States, which the Friendship and Magnanimity of your conduct towards them, afforded reason to expect.

The United States, having unanimously appointed me to the supreme executive authority, in this Nation, your Majesty's letter of the 17th of August 1788, which, by reason of the dissolution of the late Government, remained unanswered, has been delivered to me. I have also received the letters, which your Imperial Majesty has been so kind as to write, in favor of the United States, to the Bashaws of Tunis and Tripoli, and I present to you the sincere acknowledgments and thanks of the United States, for this important mark of your friendship for them.

We greatly regret that the hostile disposition of those regencies towards this Nation, who have never injured them, is not to be removed, on terms in our power to comply with. Within our territories there are no mines either of Gold or Silver, and this young Nation, just recovering from the waste and desolation of a long war, have not, as yet, had time to acquire riches by agriculture

agriculture and commerce. But our soil is bountiful, and our people industrious, and we have reason to flatter ourselves that we shall gradually become useful to our friends.

The encouragement which your Majesty has been pleased, generously, to give to our Commerce with your Dominions, the punctuality with which you have caused the Treaty with us to be observed, and the just and generous measures taken in the case of Captain Proctor, make a deep impression on the United States, and confirm their respect for and attachment to your Imperial Majesty.

It gives me pleasure to have this opportunity of assuring your Majesty that, while I remain at the head of this Nation, I shall not cease to promote every measure that may conduce to the Friendship and Harmony which so happily subsist between your Empire and them, and shall esteem myself happy in every occasion of convincing your Majesty of the high sense (which in common with the whole Nation) I entertain of the Magnanimity, Wisdom, and Benevolence of your Majesty.

In the course of the approaching winter, the national legislature (which is called by the former name of Congress) will assemble, and I shall take care that nothing be omitted that may be necessary to cause the correspondence between our two countries to be maintained and conducted in a manner agreeable to your Majesty, and satisfactory to all the parties concerned in it.

May the Almighty bless your Imperial Majesty, our great and magnanimous Friend, with his constant guidance and protection. Written at the City of New York the first day of December 1789. G^o Washington

To Our great and magnanimous Friend, his imperial majesty the Emperor of Morocco.

Letter from President George Washington to Emperor Mohammed III of Morocco, a direct ancestor of the present king, His Majesty Hassan II, who is seventeenth in the Alaouite line. The treaty mentioned is the "Treaty of Peace and Friendship" signed by Morocco and the United States in 1787 for a duration of fifty years. The treaty was renegotiated in 1836 and is still in force, constituting the longest unbroken treaty relationship in United States history.

To the Emperor of Morocco,

Great and magnanimous Friend

Since the date of the letter which the late Congress, by their President, addressed to your Imperial Majesty, the United States of America have thought proper to change their Government and to institute a new one, agreeable to the Constitution, of which I have the honor of herewith inclosing a Copy. The time necessarily employed in this arduous task, and the derangements occasioned by so great, though peaceable a Revolution, will apologize and account for your Majesty's not having received those regular advices, and marks of attention from the United States, which the Friendship and Magnanimity of your conduct towards them afforded reason to expect.

The United States, having unanimously appointed me to the supreme executive authority in this nation, your Majesty's letter of the 17th of August 1788 which, by reason of the dissolution of the late Government, remained unanswered has been delivered to me. I have also received the Letters, which your Imperial Majesty has been so kind as to write, in favor of the United States, to the Pashaws of Tunis and Tripoli, and I present to you the sincere acknowledgments and thanks of the United States for this important mark of your friendship for them.

We greatly regret that the hostile disposition of those regencies towards this nation, who have never injured them, is not to be removed on terms in our power to comply with. Within our territories there are no mines either of Gold or Silver, and this young Nation, just recovering from the Waste and Desolation of a long war, has not, as yet, had time to acquire riches by agriculture and Commerce. But our soil is bountiful, and our people industrious, and we have reason to flatter ourselves that we shall gradually become useful to our friends.

The encouragement which your Majesty has been pleased, generously, to give to our Commerce with your Dominion, the punctuality with which you have caused the Treaty with us to be observed, and the just and generous measures taken in the case of Captain Proctor make a deep impression on the United States and confirm their respect for, and attachment to your Imperial Majesty.

It gives me pleasure to have this opportunity of assuring your Majesty that, while I remain at the head of this nation, I shall not cease to promote every measure that may conduce to the Friendship and Harmony which so happily subsist between your Empire and them, and shall esteem myself happy in every occasion of convincing your Majesty of the high sense (which in common with the whole nation) I entertain of the Magnanimity, Wisdom and Benevolence of your Majesty.

In the course of the approaching winter, the national legislature (which is called by the former name of Congress) will assemble, and I shall take care that nothing be omitted that may be necessary to cause the correspondence between our two countries to be maintained and conducted in a manner agreeable to your Majesty and satisfactory to all the parties concerned in it.

May the Almighty bless your Imperial Majesty, our great and magnanimous Friend, with his constant guidance and protection.

Written at the City of New York the first day of December 1789.
(signed) G. Washington

بسم الله الرحمن الرحيم ولا حول ولا قوة إلا بالله العلي العظيم

من عبد الله محمد بن عبد الله كان الله له آمين

1202

In the name of God, the merciful.

There exists strength and power only by God.

From the Servant of God, Mohammed Ibn 'Abd Allah - may God help him - to the President of the United States of America.

Salvation be upon him who follows the Righteous Path.

We received your letter in which you propose a peace* treaty. (We are informing you that) our intention is also to maintain peaceful* relations with you. We have also contacted Tunis and Tripoli regarding what you solicited from Our Majesty** and all your requests will materialize, God willing.

Written

on the 15 Dhû al-Qa'da 1202.

* At the time this was written, the word "peace" was also used to mean friendship. The treaty discussed was a friendship treaty.

** Washington had asked the Sultan to intercede with authorities in Tunis and Tripoli to obtain the right of free navigation for American ships in the Mediterranean.

Au nom de Dieu, le miséricordieux.

La force et le pouvoir n'existent que grâce à Dieu.

Du Serviteur de Dieu, Mohammed Ibn 'Abd Allah - que Dieu l'aide - au Président des Etats-Unis d'Amérique.

Que celui qui suit la Voie Juste trouve le Salut.

Nous avons reçu votre lettre dans laquelle vous proposez un traité de paix. (Nous vous informons que) nous avons aussi l'intention de maintenir des rapports pacifiques* avec vous. Nous nous sommes adressés à Tunis et Tripoli au sujet de vos requêtes de Sa Majesté (notre monarque)** et on accédera à toutes vos requêtes, s'il plaît à Dieu.*

Ecrit

le 15 Dhû al-Qa'da 1202.

* *A l'époque où ce traité fut écrit, le mot "paix" signifiait aussi "amitié." Le traité discuté était un traité d'amitié.*

** *Washington avait demandé au Sultan d'intercéder auprès des autorités à Tunis et à Tripoli pour obtenir le droit de navigation libre pour les vaisseaux américains dans la Méditerranée.*

Embassy of the
Kingdom of Morocco
Washington, D.C.

It gives me great pleasure as Ambassador of the Kingdom of Morocco to the United States to introduce American readers to a book which I believe most skillfully captures the magic, the beauty, the hospitality, and the customs of my country. The book has been created in tribute to the great and longstanding friendship between our two countries, by an artist who is one of Morocco's dearest friends.

It is always with great pride that I recall that the friendship between the United States and Morocco dates back to the birth of the United States, when Morocco was one of the first countries to recognize the new republic. The Treaty of Peace and Friendship, ratified in 1787, is one of the oldest treaties in American history, and opened diplomatic relations between our two nations.

Indeed, we truly are neighbors, separated only by an ocean and by our limited acquaintance. It is my ardent hope that this magnificent book, with its splendid photographs and illustrations, will encourage more Americans to make the short trip across the Atlantic ocean, not only to visit, but also to explore and get to know Morocco and Moroccans. For while the images and the text reveal a country that is exotic and mysterious to Americans, I believe they also convey the warm and generous welcome that awaits you.

Mohamed Belkhayat
Ambassador

**Embassy of the
Kingdom of Morocco
Washington, D.C.**

J'ai le grand plaisir, en tant qu'ambassadeur du Royaume du Maroc aux Etats-Unis, de présenter aux lecteurs américains un livre qui reproduit avec grâce la magie, la beauté, l'hospitalité et les coutumes de mon pays. Ce livre a été écrit pour rendre hommage à la grande et longue amitié entre nos deux pays, par un artiste qui est un des plus chers amis du Maroc.

C'est toujours avec grande fierté que je me rappelle que l'amitié entre les Etats-Unis et le Maroc date de la naissance des Etats-Unis, quand le Maroc fut un des premiers pays à reconnaître la nouvelle république. Le Traité de Paix et d'Amitié, ratifié en 1787, est un des plus anciens traités de l'histoire américaine, et a ouvert les relations diplomatiques entre nos deux nations.

En effet, nous sommes vraiment voisins, séparés seulement par un océan et le fait que nous ne nous connaissons pas trop bien. C'est mon espoir ardent que ce livre magnifique, avec ses photos et illustrations splendides, encouragera plus d'Américains à traverser l'océan Atlantique non seulement pour visiter, mais aussi pour explorer et faire la connaissance du Maroc et des Marocains. Car tandis que les images et le texte révèlent un pays exotique et mystérieux pour les Américains, je crois qu'ils communiquent aussi l'accueil chaleureux et généreux qui vous y attend.

Mohamed Belkhayat
Ambassadeur

Foreword

By Alf Taylor

It was the fall of 1975 that I wandered off a boat in Tangier's harbor and first set foot on the coast of Morocco. My total worth was a backpack full of dirty laundry, enough traveler's checks to scrimp by for a couple of weeks, a plane ticket back to a boring job in a Tucson ad agency, and a pocket-sized book called *See and Point*. *See and Point* had small pictures of most of one's daily needs, in alphabetical order. To find a hotel, look under "H." The photo was unmistakably a hotel in any language. Point to the photo and someone would surely point you to a hotel, oftentimes teaching you their word for hotel. "R" for restaurant, "T" for ------... you get the picture. My *See and Point* had nursed me around Europe with a fluency, so I gave it a chance to see and point me around North Africa.

Ahhh, Morocco, at last I would get to live the Arabian Nights without being asleep. As a kid, my heroes weren't cowboys or jet pilots. I read and dreamed about desert sheiks with veiled women, and camel caravaners in jeweled turbans trading stacks of rugs and bolts of silk. To this day I have difficulty walking through the Moroccan brass markets without giving each lamp a quick rub.

Ramadan, the Islamic period of religious fasting, had just ended, and Tangier was in complete celebration. I checked into a small hotel in the Medina (the old city) and spent the first day sitting on my balcony watching the festivities. The streets were teeming with women with covered faces wearing silk and gold lamé caftans in every conceivable color, businessmen in high fashion French suits, others in hooded jellabas woven so finely that they were transparent. Off to my left, a new Mercedes idled patiently while two donkey carts navigated their way around. Across the street, in front of a café, a woman lifted her veil high enough to take a sip from a bottle of Pepsi. Beneath my window, a

Préface

par Alf Taylor

C'était en automne de 1975 que j'ai débarqué sans but d'un bateau dans le port de Tanger et que j'ai mis pied pour la première fois sur le rivage du Maroc. Mes possessions totales comprenaient un sac à dos plein de linge sale, assez de chèques de voyage pour lésiner pendant deux ou trois semaines, un billet d'avion de retour à un travail ennuyeux dans une agence de publicité à Tucson, et un livre de poche intitulé See and Point. See and Point *(voyez et montrez du doigt) contenait des petites images de la plupart des besoins quotidiens, en ordre alphabétique. Pour trouver un hôtel, il fallait regarder sous "H." La photo représentait indubitablement un hôtel dans n'importe quelle langue. Montrez la photo du doigt, et quelqu'un vous indiquera sûrement un hôtel, souvent en vous disant le mot "hôtel" dans leur langue. Cherchez sous "R" pour restaurant, "T" pour -------...vous voyez comment ça marche. Mon* See and Point *m'a entretenu tout autour de l'Europe avec une certaine aisance, alors je lui ai donné occasion de me faire voir et montrer du doigt l'Afrique du Nord.*

Aaah, le Maroc, enfin je vivrai les mille et une nuits sans être endormi. Quand j'étais enfant, mes héros n'étaient pas les cowboys ou les pilotes de jets. Je lisais et rêvais de cheiks du désert et de femmes voilées, et de voyageurs de caravanes en turbans ornés de bijoux, vendant des piles de tapis et des rouleaux de soie. Jusqu'à ce jour, j'ai de la difficulté à traverser les marchés de laiton marocains sans donner un coup de chiffon rapide à chaque lampe.

Le ramadan, la période islamique de jeûne religieux, venait de finir et Tanger était en pleine célébration. Je remplis une fiche à un petit hôtel dans la médine (la vieille ville) et je passai le premier jour à mon balcon à regarder les festivités. Les rues grouillaient de monde...de femmes aux visages voilés habillées de caftans de soie et de lamé doré de toutes les couleurs imaginables, d'hommes d'affaires dans des costumes français de la dernière mode, d'autres en djellabas à capuchon tissés si délicatement qu'ils étaient transparents. A ma gauche, une nouvelle Mercedes tournait patiemment au ralenti tandis que deux charrettes à ânes la contournaient. De l'autre côté de la rue, devant un café, une femme soulevait son voile juste assez pour boire une petite gorgée d'une bouteille de Pepsi. Sous ma fenêtre, un

man in a big red hat was selling water by the cup, ringing a bell so that all who wanted a drink or a photo would know his whereabouts. The squeal of a snake charmer's flute invaded my room. (How could a sound I had never heard before be so instantly recognizable?) I could smell the mint as it was shifted from the back of a motorscooter to the grocer's scales, and bread so fresh that one could find the bakery blindfolded. My senses were on fire. Morocco's exotic splendor had paled my childhood dreams.

Day two, 6:00 AM, and time to hit the souks (marketplace). The streets were already filled with the laughter of school children. Rows of sliding metal doors were disappearing, exposing shops so full of goods that the merchants had to sit outside. Waiters in sidewalk cafés were serving croissants and café au lait at a frenzied pace. And everybody, I mean everybody, was greeting the day and each other with an exuberance that drew me in: "Bonjour," "Sabah al-khayr" (good morning), "Labas?" (How are you?) "Labas l-hamdu-l-llah" (I'm fine, thank God), as they shook hands, followed by touching their heart or a kiss on both cheeks. My *See and Point* couldn't serve me here. Fortunately, smiles and shrugs are universal.

I wanted to see everything, taste every food, and track every sound. I wanted to skip sleep. Most of all, I wanted to buy something. But what? There was too much stuff and I had too "shwiya de-l-flus" (little money). What I needed was a *See and Point* for shopping. (Perhaps that thought was the seed for *A Treasure Hunter's Guide to Morocco.*) Before long I was approached by a Moroccan gentleman out for a walk with his grandchildren. I'm sure my dazed look said that I was fresh off the boat. He talked to me in broken English about Tangier and life in Morocco. By "coincidence," he had a cousin with a shop full of wonderful things: we walked. I'm not certain how closely the two men were related, but his description of the shop was most accurate. Without a doubt I had found Ali Baba's treasure trove. It was okay that my knees got weak because I instantly heard, "Sit, sit, sit! Coffee? Tea? Coca?" Almost before I could answer, all of these drinks were in front of me, along with a dish of freshly baked cookies. Delicious! Hanging on the wall was a magnificent leather bag covered with old coins. "How much?" I blurted out, then held my breath. "Blati," (wait) said the shopkeeper, "I have many things to show you. Then we can make one price for all."

The merchant moved with the agility of a matador as he whirled rugs and tapestries at my feet. The sound of a hundred or more bracelets and rings poured onto a glass shelf made me jump. "Shuf," (look) boasted my host, "argent!" (Silver). One of his young assistants draped a magnificent red cape over my shoulders and put a fez (tasseled Moroccan hat) on my head. A pair of matching daggers were thrust into my hands as if a cue to join his performance. He had redefined the word "overwhelmed."

A few pots of mint tea later, I had a stack of selected treasures in front of me high enough to sign my traveler's checks on. So what if I had to cut my vacation short? I wanted to ditch my clothes, stuff my backpack full, and head for the border. I had jumped into a shopping whirlwind. It was intoxicating. Suddenly, something told me to stop, that I was too far from home to be broke, that I should leave this booty behind and see Morocco. Feeling guilty for not buying, and receiving no encouragement to the contrary from either cousin, I backed out the door, pen and checkbook in hand, a little wiser and ready to head south to explore this beautiful, friendly country called Morocco.

Many years and trips later, I find myself, with the help of my friends and associates, producing a book on Morocco, specifically on many of the reasons for visiting the country, and on how to control the whirlwind of shopping excitement that awaits you there: a "See and Point" for Treasure Hunters.

My hopes are that *A Treasure Hunter's Guide to Morocco* will bridge the communication gap between artisan and patron, help stimulate and preserve Moroccan culture through the traditional arts, and make your visit to Morocco easier, more fun, and who knows, maybe even profitable.

Good Luck.

homme en grand chapeau rouge vendait de l'eau à la tasse en sonnant une clochette pour que tous ceux qui voulaient à boire ou une photo sauraient où le trouver. Le hurlement de la flute d'un charmeur de serpents envahit ma chambre. (Comment se fait-il que j'ai reconnu immédiatement un son que je n'avais jamais entendu auparavant?) Je pouvais sentir la menthe comme on la transférait de l'arrière d'un scooter à la balance d'un épicier...et le pain si frais qu'on pouvait trouver la boulangerie les yeux bandés. Mes sens étaient en flammes. La splendeur exotique du Maroc avait fait pâlir mes rêves d'enfance.

Le deuxième jour, à six heures du matin, il était temps de visiter les souks (marchés). Les rues résonnaient déjà des rires des écoliers. Des rangées de portes en métal coulissantes disparaissaient, exposant des magasins si pleins de marchandises que les marchands devaient s'asseoir dehors. Les serveurs dans les cafés le long des trottoirs servaient des croissants et du café au lait à une allure frénétique. Et tout le monde, vraiment tout le monde, saluait la journée et les uns les autres avec une exubérance attirante: "Bonjour," "Sabah al-khayr"; "Labas?" (Comment allez-vous?) "Labas l-hamdu-l-llah" (Je vais bien, Dieu merci) en se serrant les mains, et ensuite en touchant leur coeur ou en s'embrassant sur les deux joues. Mon See and Point ne pouvait pas me servir ici. Heureusement, les sourires et les haussements d'épaules sont universels.

Je voulais tout voir, goûter de chaque aliment, et suivre la piste de chaque son. Je voulais me passer de sommeil. Et surtout, je voulais acheter quelque chose. Mais quoi? Il y avait trop de choses et j'avais trop "chouiya de-l-flus" (peu d'argent). Ce qu'il me fallait, c'était un See and Point pour faire les achats. (Cette pensée fut peut-être la germe du Guide du Maroc pour les chasseurs de trésors.) Bientôt un monsieur marocain en promenade avec ses petits-enfants s'approcha de moi. Mon regard hébété disait sans doute que je venais de débarquer. Il me parla de Tanger et de la vie au Maroc, en mauvais anglais. Par "coïncidence," il avait un cousin qui possédait un magasin rempli de choses merveilleuses. Nous y sommes allés à pied. Je ne suis pas sûr qu'ils étaient proches parents, mais sa description du magasin était très exacte. J'avais certainement trouvé le trésor d'Ali Baba. Ce n'était pas un problème que mes genoux se dérobaient, parce qu'on me dit tout de suite "Asseyez-vous, asseyez-vous, asseyez-vous! Café? Thé? Coca?" Presque avant que je puisse répondre, toutes ces boissons étaient devant moi, avec un plat de biscuits tous frais du four. Quelles délices! Un magnifique sac en cuir recouvert d'anciennes pièces de monnaie était suspendu au mur. "Combien?" je jetai, puis je retins mon souffle. "Blati," (attend) dit le marchand, "j'ai plusieurs choses à te montrer. Ensuite nous pouvons décider d'un prix pour tout."

Le marchand remuait avec l'agilité d'un matador en tournoyant des tapis et des tapissseries à mes pieds. Le son d'au moins une centaine de bracelets et de bagues versés sur un rayon en verre me fit sursauter. "Chouf," (regarde) se vanta mon hôte, "argent!" Un de ses jeunes assistants drapa une magnifique cape rouge autour de mes épaules et mit un fez (calotte marocaine ornée d'un gland) sur ma tête. On me fourra dans les mains une paire de dagues assorties comme pour me signaler de me joindre à son jeu. Il avait redéfini le mot "submergé."

Après quelques pots de thé à la menthe, j'avais devant moi une pile de trésors si haute que je pouvais signer mes chèques de voyage dessus. Que m'importais si je devais couper court mon voyage? Je voulais abandonner mes habits, bourrer mon sac à dos et me diriger vers la frontière. J'avais sauté dans une tornade d'achats. C'était enivrant. Soudain, quelque chose me dit de m'arrêter, que j'étais trop loin de chez moi pour être fauché, sans le sou, que je devrais laisser ce butin et voir le Maroc. Ayant honte de n'avoir rien acheté, et comme ni l'un ni l'autre des cousins ne m'encourageait de faire le contraire, je sortis par la porte à reculons, ma plume et mon carnet de chèques en main, un peu plus sage, et prêt à me diriger vers le Sud pour explorer ce beau pays amical qu'on appelle le Maroc.

Plusieurs années et plusieurs voyages plus tard, je me trouve en train de produire, avec l'aide de mes amis et associés, un livre sur le Maroc, et spécifiquement sur beaucoup des raisons pour visiter ce pays, et sur la meilleure façon de contrôler cette fièvre de faire les achats qui vous attend là-bas: un "See and Point" pour les chasseurs de trésors.

J'espère que le Guide du Maroc pour les chasseurs de trésors va diminuer l'écart entre l'artisan et le protecteur, et va aider à stimuler et préserver la culture marocaine par l'intermédiaire de ses arts traditionnels, tout en rendant votre visite au Maroc plus facile, plus amusante, et qui le sait, peut-être même avantageuse.

Bonne chance.

Photo: Hahn

Ensemble Artisanal, place des Oudaias, Rabat.
Ensemble Artisanal, place des Oudaias, Rabat.

Ensemble Artisanal

It is difficult to imagine visiting Morocco without spending some time in Rabat, the capital of Morocco and the home of the Royal Family. Rabat contains a wealth of Moroccan culture.

For a good overview of the contemporary Moroccan handicraft industry, you must tour the Ensemble Artisanal. Here you will find assembled artisans plying their trade in every medium. Items can be purchased directly from the artists. If you have an idea about something that you would like produced in Morocco, you will find the Artisanal staff most accommodating: For one piece or a thousand, the Ensemble Artisanal is a good place to stop.

My thanks to Mr. Hihi at the Ensemble Artisanal for escorting me through it and allowing me to photograph the facility.

L'Ensemble Artisanal

Il est difficile d'imaginer une visite au Maroc sans passer du temps à Rabat, la capitale du Maroc et la ville où réside la Famille Royale. Rabat contient une abondance d'expressions de la culture marocaine.

Pour un bon aperçu de l'industrie artisanale marocaine contemporaine, il faut faire le tour de l'Ensemble Artisanal. Là vous trouverez un groupe d'artisans pratiquant leur métier par tous les moyens d'expression artisanale. Vous pouvez acheter les articles directement des artistes. S'il y a quelque chose que vous aviez l'idée de faire produire sur commande au Maroc, vous trouverez que le personnel de l'Ensemble Artisanal est très obligeant: pour un article ou pour mille, l'Ensemble Artisanal est l'endroit à visiter.

Je voudrais remercier M. Hihi de l'Ensemble Artisanal de m'avoir accompagné tout autour de l'installation et de m'avoir donné la permission de la photographier.

Photo: Hahn

Leather craftsman: Slippers and poufs (cushions). Ensemble Artisanal, Rabat.
Maroquinier: pantoufles et poufs. Ensemble Artisanal, Rabat.

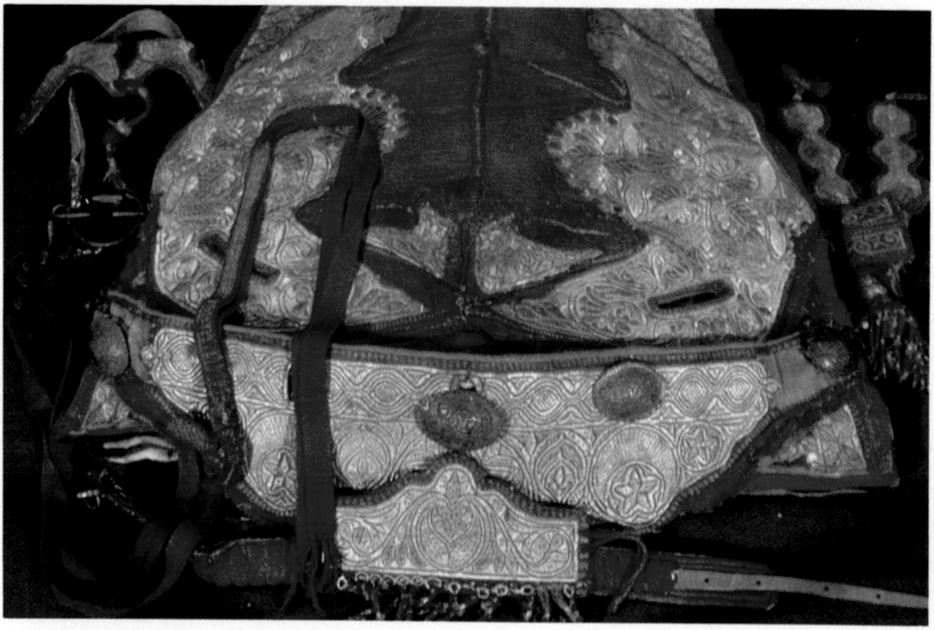

Photo: Sisk

Saddle: Leather, silk and silver, 19th Century. AMMA.
Selle: cuir, soie et argent, 19ème siècle. AMMA.

Photo: Hahn

Craftsman of Moroccan shoes (babouches). Ensemble Artisanal, Rabat.
Fabriquant de chaussures marocaines (babouches). Ensemble Artisanal, Rabat.

Photo: Sisk

Antique leather bag. AMMA.
Ancien sac en cuir. AMMA.

Photo: Hahn

Leather craftsman: Bookbindings, portfolios, picture frames etc. Ensemble Artisanal, Rabat.
Maroquinier: reliures, portefeuilles, cadres, etc. Ensemble Artisanal, Rabat.

Photo: Hahn

Leather craftsman: Purses, briefcases, carrying bags. Ensemble Artisanal, Rabat.
Maroquinier: sacs à main, serviettes, sacs. Ensemble Artisanal, Rabat.

Photo: Hahn

Mosaic tile artists. Ensemble Artisanal, Rabat. *Artistes de zelliges. Ensemble Artisanal, Rabat.*

Photo: Hahn

Hand-carved plaster, wood and tile mosque doors, next to the Tomb of Mohammed V, Rabat.
Portes de mosquée en stuc, bois et zelliges ouvragées à la main, à côté du tombeau de Mohammed V, Rabat.

The carpenters' fountain, Fez.
La fontaine des menuisiers, Fès.

Music and Musical Instruments
Musique et instruments de musique

Gnaoua musician and son, Marrakesh. Photo: Author
Un musicien de Gnaoua et son fils, Marrakech.

Photo: Sisk

Moroccan guitar and thumb percussion. AMMA.
Guitare et percussion marocaines. AMMA.

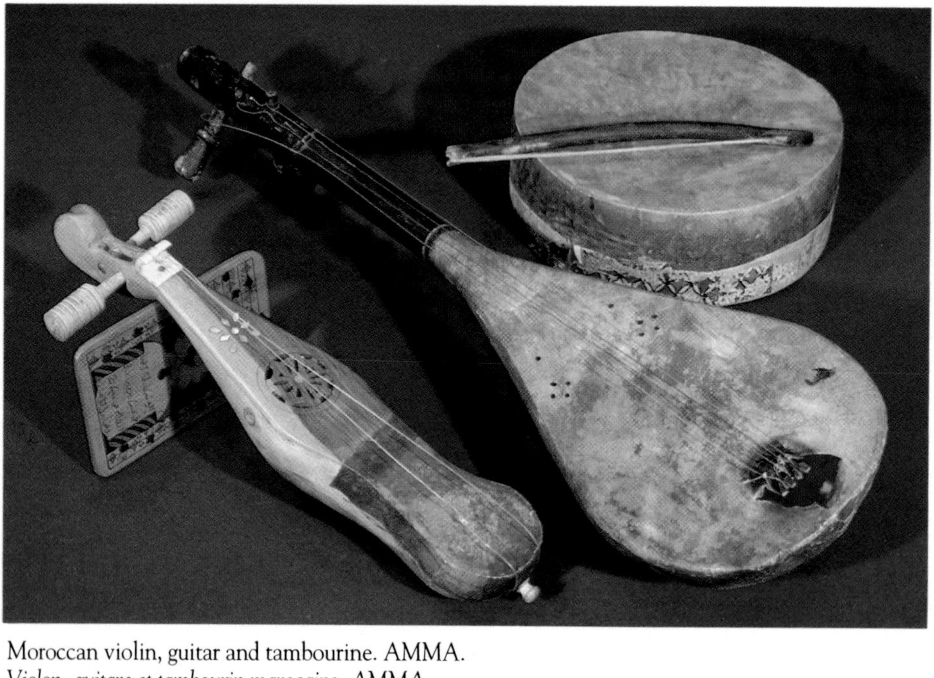

Photo: Sisk

Moroccan violin, guitar and tambourine. AMMA.
Violon, guitare et tambourin marocains. AMMA.

Photo: Hahn

Musicians from the south. Chellah Gardens, Rabat.
Musiciens du Sud. Jardins de Chellah, Rabat.

Photo: Sisk

Pottery and wooden drums, snake charmers' flutes. AMMA.
Tambours en céramique et en bois, flûtes de charmeurs de serpents. AMMA.

Photo: Hahn

Metalwork. Musée National de l'Artisanat, Rabat.
Ferronnerie. Musée national de l'Artisanat, Rabat.

Photo: Hahn

Brass and copper market, Marrakesh.
Marché de cuivre et de laiton, Marrakech.

Photo: Hahn

Lampmaker. Ensemble Artisanal, Rabat. *Fabricant de lampes. Ensemble Artisanal, Rabat.*

Photo: Author

Judi Taylor with spice vendor, Marrakesh.
Judi Taylor avec un vendeur d'épices, Marrakech.

The Spice Markets

"Perhaps Madam would like to smell this saffron, yes?" asks the spice merchant, as he casually scoops out more of the golden spice than most people see in a lifetime. "I also have cumin, amber, sandalwood, patchouli and pure musk. Look around you. I have so much," he says, handing you objects to inspect as he speaks. Small pottery dishes that melt into liquid rouge when touched by moisture, natural-stem toothpicks still on the pod, green lipstick that appears red on the lips, incense from many parts of the world: Marco Polo could have saved a lot of time here.

The spice markets of Morocco are fascinating, and the spice merchants are like nature's pharmacists. The smallest amount of money will buy the most interesting souvenirs. These markets can be found in most cities… just open to this page and point.

Les marchés d'épices

"Est-ce que Madame voudrait renifler ce safran, oui?" demande le vendeur d'épices, en ramassant avec désinvolture plus de cette épice dorée que la plupart des gens n'aient vu de leur vie. "J'ai aussi du cumin, de l'ambre, du santal, du patchouli et du musc pur. Regardez autour de vous. J'ai tant de choses à vendre," dit-il en vous tendant des objets à inspecter. Des petits pots de céramique qui se fondent en rouge liquide en contact avec l'humidité, des cure-dents encore attachés à leurs tiges naturelles, du rouge à lèvres vert qui devient rouge sur les lèvres, de l'encens provenant de plusieurs parties du monde: Marco Polo aurait gagné beaucoup de temps ici.

Les marchés d'épices du Maroc sont fascinants, et les marchands d'épices ressemblent à des pharmaciens naturels. Des toutes petites sommes d'argent vous payeront des souvenirs très intéressants. Ces marchés se trouvent dans la plupart des villes…ouvrez tout simplement ce livre à cette page et indiquez-la du doigt.

There is no spell as sweet as that induced by
The Children's Rugs of Central Morocco

Handwoven by the mothers and young women of the Berber tribes with children in mind, the children's rugs of Central Morocco personify the word "delightful." Contemporary dyes and non-traditional designs are coupled with fine wools and cottons (and some rayon) to create these whimsical masterpieces. In the designs you'll find every kind of animal you ever knew… plus some you've never dreamed of, rows of children holding hands, automobiles with two rear ends, tractors, houses or tents, and pictorial stories about events in the family's life. The list is as endless as the weavers' imaginations, and each piece is unique.

The Children's Rugs can be found in any of the major cities, but for a "fresh from the loom" selection, I suggest a visit to one of the country markets between Rabat and Fez: Khemisset on Tuesday or Tiflet on Wednesday. Go early. If you take pictures, get your photo subjects' addresses in Morocco so you can share your photos with them.

Il n'y a pas de charme aussi doux que celui des
petits tapis d'enfants du Maroc central

Tissés à la main pour les enfants par les mères et jeunes femmes des tribus berbères, les tapis d'enfants du Maroc central sont le délice personnifié. Des teintures contemporaines et des motifs non-traditionnels sont combinés avec la laine et le coton fins (et un peu de rayonne) pour créer ces chefs-d'oeuvre fantaisistes. Vous trouverez dans les motifs toutes les espèces d'animaux imaginables…en plus de certaines que vous n'avez jamais imaginées, et des rangées d'enfants la main dans la main, des voitures avec deux bouts arrières, des maisons ou des tentes, et des images racontant des événements de la vie de la famille. La liste n'est limitée que par l'imagination des tisserandes, et chaque tapis est unique.

On peut trouver des tapis d'enfants dans toutes les villes principales, mais pour un choix de tapis tout droit du métier, je vous suggère de visiter un des marchés ruraux entre Rabat et Fès: Khemisset les mardis ou Tiflet les mercredis. Allez-y de bonne heure. Si vous prenez des photos, demandez les adresses de ceux que vous avez photographiés pour pouvoir leur en envoyer une copie.

Photo: Author

Left to right: Twin Youssef, Fatimzohra, Zineb, Ihsane, Sidi Mohamed, Twin Miriam. Marrakesh.
De gauche à droite: frère jumeau Youssef, Fatimzohra, Zineb, Ihsane, Sidi Mohamed, soeur jumelle Miriam. Marrakech.

Photo: Walker

Melika and Karima, Berber children of Tiflet.
Melika et Karima, enfants berbères de Tiflet.

Photo: Sisk

Children's rug: Hitchhiking chickens.
Petit tapis d'enfants: poulets faisant de l'auto-stop.

Photo: Author

Sadie the dancing dog and Shanti the soprano. Children's rug: smiling lions. AMMA.
Sadie, le chien qui danse, et Shanti, la soprano. Petit tapis d'enfants: lions souriants. AMMA.

Photo: J. Taylor

Hadj Omar, a fine textile merchant of Marrakesh, and the author.
Hadj Omar, un marchand de textiles fins de Marrakech, et l'auteur.

Strike your Own Bargain: The Art of Gentle Persuasion

"Look into my eyes Hadj Omar, my good friend, and tell me your very best price," I say. "Give me what you offered, plus 100 dirhams more for my profit," Hadj replies. I comply. Then there is tea drinking and a lot of ceremony to celebrate a good deal for all.

Morocco is the epitome of free enterprise and Moroccans are born negotiators. While most hotels and other tourist-related industries have fixed prices, bargaining is a natural part of shopping here. When I meet someone who has visited Morocco, questions about shopping usually arise. "Did I pay too much for this?" they ask. Or, "How much would this cost back home?" and so on. My answers are instinctual: "You bought it. Obviously it must have been worth what you paid, to you, and that's what matters." And, "Most likely you couldn't buy it back home at all." Just don't buy anything you don't like, and you'll always be happy.

As a general rule, purchases you make while bargaining will be fun or luxury items that you don't need at all. In most cases they will be worth at least what you pay, and much more than what your money would buy back home. It's this rule that keeps me in the import business.

There are many banks and currency exchange offices where you can change your money to Moroccan dirhams. It's likely that your hotel will offer this service, and initially, the Casablanca airport is a good place for this. Save your currency change receipts. Do not change currency on the street: It is against the law. Credit cards are accepted in most places, and offer you added protection.

I suggest that if you find an old silver ring that you like, buy it for the ring, not the "old" or "silver." Chances are that even the vendor doesn't know the ring's origin or metal content. That way, you won't be disappointed.

The bargaining game can be fun and exciting if you approach it with a good attitude. The merchant has a right to ask any price he likes for his merchandise. As a player, you have a right to refuse, or to make any offer you please. If your offer comes close to matching his price, you will most likely strike a deal. Keep in mind that just as you do not want to pay too much, you also don't have to beat someone down to their lowest price to achieve a "good deal." A good deal is when both parties come away happy. Play the game often. Your skills will improve quickly... and the memories you make will last forever.

I'll leave you with three thoughts: you're in Morocco as a guest of all of the Moroccan people; have fun and shop a lot; and the word "beware" derives from "be aware."

Concluez votre propre marché: l'art de la persuasion

"Regarde-moi dans les yeux, Hadj Omar, mon cher ami, et dis-moi ton meilleur prix," je dis. "Donne-moi ce que tu m'as offert, et 100 dirhams de plus pour mon profit," répond Hadj. J'accepte, et ensuite nous buvons du thé et nous faisons beaucoup de cérémonies pour fêter une bonne affaire pour tous.

Le Maroc est l'exemple même de la libre enterprise et les Marocains sont des négotiateurs nés. Bien que la plupart des hôtels et autres industries connexes au tourisme aient des prix fixes, le marchandage fait partie tout naturellement du commerce ici. Quand je rencontre quelqu'un qui a visité le Maroc, il ou elle me pose d'habitude des questions concernant les achats. "Est-ce que j'ai payé ça trop cher?" on me demande, ou bien "combien ça coûterait chez nous?" et ainsi de suite. Je réponds instinctivement: "Vous l'avez acheté. Evidemment, vous avez dû trouver que ça valait le prix que vous avez payé, et c'est ça qui compte." Et aussi, "vous ne pourriez sans doute pas trouver cela chez vous du tout." Il ne faut simplement pas acheter quelque chose qui ne vous plaît pas, et vous serez toujours satisfaits.

En règle générale, les achats que vous ferez en marchandant seront des articles amusants ou de luxe dont vous n'avez pas du tout besoin. Dans la plupart des cas, leur valeur sera au moins égale au prix que vous payerez, et bien supérieure au prix vous auriez payé chez vous. C'est pour cela que je reste dans l'importation.

Il y a beaucoup de banques et de bureaux de change de devises où vous pourrez convertir votre argent en dirhams marocains. Votre hôtel offrira sans doute ce service, et vous pourrez changer votre argent à l'aéroport de Casablanca en arrivant. Gardez vos reçus de change. Ne changez pas vos devises dans la rue: c'est interdit. On accepte les cartes de crédit dans la plupart des endroits, et elles vous fourniront de la sécurité supplémentaire.

Si vous trouvez une vieille bague en argent qui vous plaît, je vous conseille de l'acheter parce qu'elle vous plaît, et non pas parce qu'elle est "vieille" ou "en argent." Il est probable que même le vendeur ne connait ni l'origine de la bague, ni sa teneur en métal. Ainsi, vous ne serez pas déçus.

Le jeu du marchandage peut être amusant et excitant si vous l'abordez avec une bonne attitude. Le marchand a le droit de demander n'importe quel prix pour ses marchandises. Comme joueurs, vous avez le droit de refuser ou de lui offrir n'importe quelle somme. Si votre offre se rapproche de son prix, vous allez sans doute faire une affaire. Souvenez-vous que tout en ne pas voulant payer trop, vous n'êtes pas non plus obligés d'arriver au prix le plus bas pour faire une "bonne affaire." Une bonne affaire, c'est quand les deux intéressés sont satisfaits. Jouez ce jeu souvent. Votre deviendrez vite plus habiles...et vous aurez des souvenirs pour toute la vie.

Je vous laisse avec trois pensées: vous êtes au Maroc comme hôtes du peuple marocain; amusez-vous et faites beaucoup d'achats; et soyez conscients et prudents.

Photo:Author

Everyone bargains, everyone has fun.
Tout le monde marchande, tout le monde s'amuse.

Thank You Ali Bengelloun

From all of the Americans and Moroccans who have benefitted from his support of the arts and cultural exchange programs, our thanks and respects to Former Moroccan Ambassador to the United States, His Excellency Ali Bengelloun.

Merci beaucoup Ali Bengelloun

Nous voudrions exprimer nos remerciements et notre respect à Son Excellence, Monsieur Ali Bengelloun, ancien ambassadeur du Royaume du Maroc aux Etats-Unis, de la part de tous les Américains et Marocains qui ont bénéficié de son soutien aux arts et aux programmes d'échanges culturels.

Photo: Hahn

Lathe worker. Ensemble Artisanal, Rabat.
Travailleur au tour. Ensemble Artisanal, Rabat.

Photo: Sisk

Koranic Scripture boards. The back is used for children's tablets.
Tableau d'Ecritures coraniques. Le dos sert de tableau à écrire pour enfants.

Photo: Hampton

The foot lathe artists make beautiful souvenirs. Marrakesh.
Les artistes du tour marchant au pied fabriquent des beaux souvenirs. Marrakech.

Photo: Sisk

Antique trunk: Wood, leather, brass and copper, 19th Century. AMMA.
Ancien coffre: bois, cuir, laiton et cuivre, 19ème siècle. AMMA.

Photo: Author

Wood craftsmen of Essaouira. Berber Bazaar.
Marqueteurs d'Essaouira. Bazar berbère.

Photo: Sisk

Antique inlaid desk: Ivory and mother of pearl, 19th Century. AMMA.
Ancien bureau marqueté: ivoire et nacre, 19ème siècle. AMMA.

Photo: Sisk

Inlaid table and box from Essaouira. Old Pueblo Museum.
Table et boîte incrustées d'Essaouira. Old Pueblo Museum.

Photo: J. Taylor

The author acquiring an old door for exhibition and book *Doors of the Moors*.
L'auteur se procurant une vieille porte pour l'exhibition et le livre Portes des Maures.

Tailors, Exotic Fabrics and Costumes of Morocco-Oudaias, Museum, Rabat
Les tailleuses, les tissus exotiques et Costumes du Maroc-Musée des Oudaias

Photo: Hahn

Tailor and embroideress. Ensemble Artisanal, Rabat.
Tailleuse et brodeuse. Ensemble Artisanal, Rabat.

Photo: Author

Judi Taylor and Sarmi Hind search the fabric market for silks and lamé. Marrakesh.
Judi Taylor et Sarmi Hind fouillent le marché de tissus à la recherche de la soie et du lamé. Marrakech.

Photo: Author

Traditional handmade caftan: Caftans by Hind. Marrakesh.
Caftan traditionnel fait à la main: Caftans de Hind. Marrakech.

Photo: Author

Costume of Tiznit, Museum of the Oudaias, Rabat.
Costume de Tiznit, Musée des Oudaias, Rabat.

Photo: Author

Costume of Ida Ounadif, Museum of the Oudaias, Rabat.
Costume de Ida Ounadif, Musée des Oudaias, Rabat.

Photo: Author

Costume of Ait Sherouchen, Sahara. Museum of the Oudaias, Rabat.
Costume de Ait Sherouchen, Sahara. Musée des Oudaias, Rabat.

Photo: Author

Costume of the Rif. Museum of the Oudaias, Rabat.
Costume du Rif. Musée des Oudaias, Rabat.

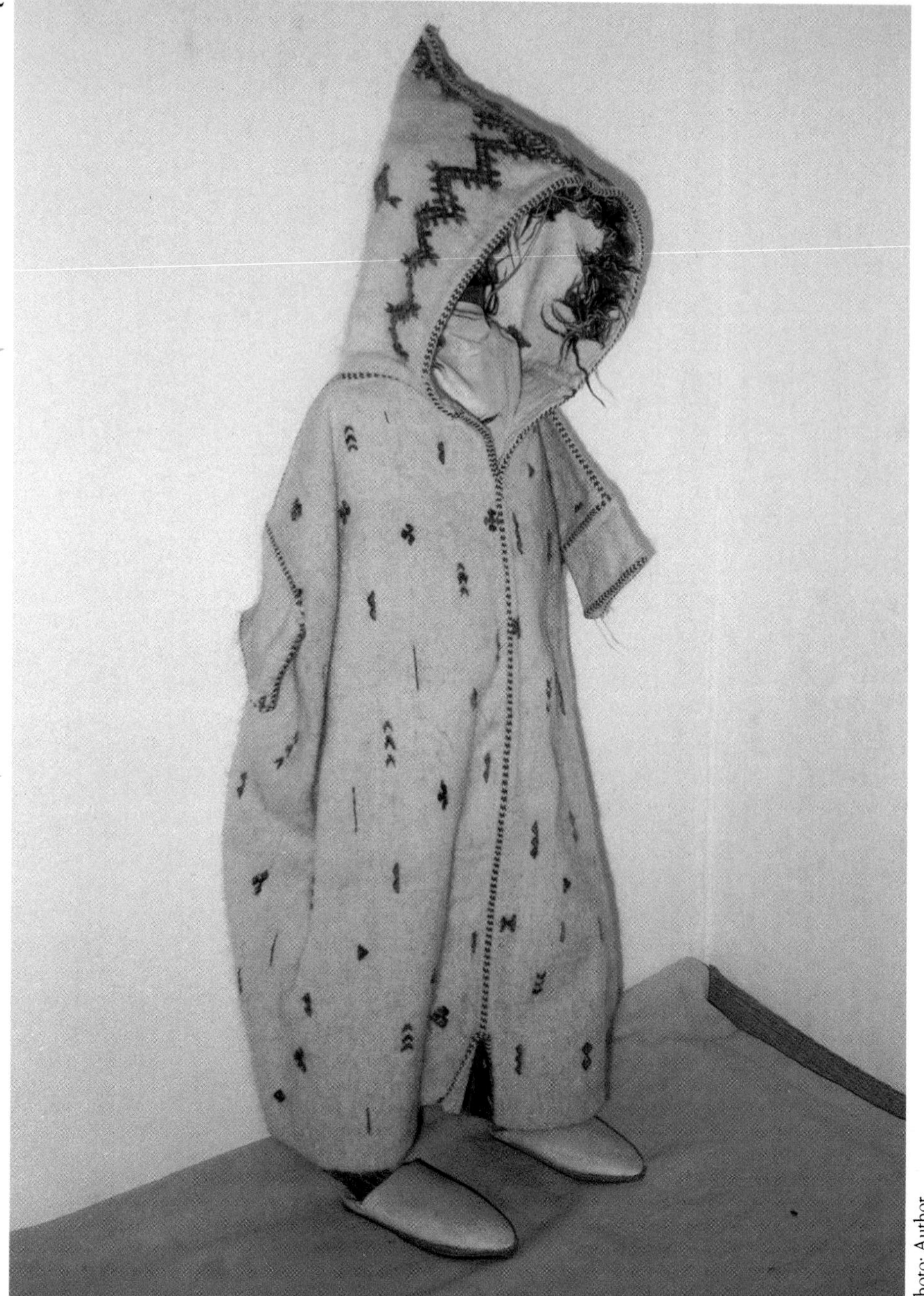

Photo: Author

Child's jellaba. Museum of the Oudaias, Rabat.
Djellaba d'enfant. Musée des Oudaias, Rabat.

Moroccan Cooking

A Moroccan meal often begins with someone coming to your table with a basin, a bar of soap and a towel, so you can wash your hands. When eating at home, the head of the household will say "Bismillah" (praise be to God).

COUSCOUS: This is the national dish, generally made of wheat semolina steamed over lamb or chicken stew, with vegetables and garbanzo beans. Couscous preparation varies from region to region: they eat a seven-course couscous in Casablanca, etc. Couscous is traditionally eaten with the fingers, but the use of spoons is becoming more and more common.

MESHOUI: Oven-roasted or barbecued lamb: the impaled lamb, supported by two forks, is usually set at a certain height in the fire. This succulent dish is usually served at the beginning of a feast.

BASTILLA: Thin flaky pastry stuffed with pigeon or chicken, and almonds.

TAJINES: Lamb or poultry stew, garnished with olives, almonds or prunes.

HARIRA: A thick soup with small meat cubes, lentils, garbanzo beans, tomatoes, and exotic spices specific to this dish.

BEVERAGES: Tea, the national drink, is served in glasses at all times and everywhere. It has a mint flavor and is very sweet. It is sometimes also seasoned with orange blossoms.

Sidi Ali, Sidi Harazem and Oulmas are good bottled waters, with or without carbonation.

PASTRIES: Lots of honey and almonds. The "gazelle horn," a crescent-shaped almond pastry, is delicious.

MILK AND DATES: A symbol of Moroccan hospitality.

I would like to thank the Moroccan National Tourist Office and Rafih Bengelloun of the Imperial Fez Moroccan Restaurant in Vail, Colorado, USA, for this information on Moroccan cooking.

La cuisine marocaine

Un repas marocain commence souvent après que quelqu'un ait apporté à votre table un bassin, du savon et une serviette pour que vous puissiez vous laver les mains. Quand les gens mangent chez eux, le chef de la famille dira d'abord "Bismillah" (Dieu soit loué!).

COUSCOUS: *C'est le plat national, consistant généralement de semoule de blé cuite à la vapeur combinée avec du ragoût d'agneau ou de poulet, des légumes et des pois chiches. La préparation du couscous varie d'une région à l'autre: par exemple, on mange le couscous à sept plats à Casablanca, etc. On le mange traditionnellement avec les doigts, mais on commence de plus en plus à utiliser des cuillers actuellement.*

MESHOUI: *L'agneau rôti au four ou grillé: l'agneau empalé, soutenu par deux fourches, est placé à une certaine hauteur au-dessus du feu. D'ordinaire, ce plat succulent est servi au début d'un repas.*

BASTILLA: *Fine pâtisserie feuilletée bourrée de pigeon ou de poulet, et d'amandes.*

TAJINES: *Ragoût d'agneau ou de poulet garni d'olives, d'amandes ou de prunes.*

HARIRA: *Une soupe épaisse avec des petits cubes de viande, lentilles, pois chiches, fèves, tomates, et des épices exotiques spécifiques à ce plat.*

BOISSONS: *On sert le thé, la boisson nationale, dans des verres tout le temps et partout. Ce thé parfumé à la menthe est très sucré. Il est parfois assaisonné de fleurs d'oranger.*

Sidi Ali, Sidi Harazem et Oulmas sont de bonnes eaux en bouteille gazeuses et non gazeuses.

PATISSERIES: *Elles contiennent beaucoup de miel et d'amandes. La "corne de gazelle," une pâtisserie aux amandes en forme de croissant, est délicieuse.*

LAIT ET DATES: *Un symbole de l'hospitalité marocaine.*

Je voudrais remercier l'Office National Marocain de Tourisme et Rafih Bengelloun du Imperial Fez Moroccan Restaurant à Vail, Colorado, aux Etats-Unis, de ces informations sur la cuisine marocaine.

Photo: Author

Bakers of bread, Marrakesh.
Boulangers, Marrakech.

Photo: Hahn

Restaurant. Casablanca.
Restaurant. Casablanca.

Photo: Hahn

Tea vendor, Fez. *Vendeur de thé, Fès.*

Photo: Hahn

Basket and woven furniture market, Rabat.
Marché de paniers et de meubles de vannerie, Rabat.

Photo: J. Taylor

Basket weavers and dye sellers, Marrakesh.
Vanniers et vendeurs de teintures, Marrakech.

Photo: Author

Basket seller of Marrakesh: Great baskets, a necessity for shoppers.
Vendeuse de paniers de Marrakech: d'excellents paniers, une nécessité pour ceux qui font les courses.

Photo: Duane Bryers

Dee Bryers with camera-shy boy, Rabat.
Dee Bryers avec un garçon timide.

Artists of the American West in Morocco

by Dee Bryers

Morocco has been firing the imaginations of European artists since long before Matisse's sojourn in Tangier in 1911 and 1912. Matisse's paintings of the odalisques and of the Moroccan woman Zorah were preceded by the passionate expressions of Fortuny in 1863, and by Delacroix's works in the early 1800's. Numerous other painters have also depicted Morocco's charm and mystique.

When Alf Taylor invited a group of nationally recognized western painters to tour Morocco as his guests in September 1984, they accepted with understandable eagerness. Duane Bryers, Joe Bohler, Nancy Boren, Gerald Fritzler, David Halbach, Tom Hill and Kenneth Riley are all members of prestigious art organizations, including the National Academy of Western Artists, the Cowboy Artists of America and the American Watercolor Society. Dee Bryers and artists Barbara Hill and Marcyne Riley accompanied their husbands on this expedition to do some painting, as well as to indulge in some shopping.

From the moment the painters saw the colorful harbor in Rabat bathed in golden sunlight on the evening of their arrival, their creative talents were stimulated by the provocative sights and sounds of Morocco: Dazzling displays of horsemanship at the Fantasia in Fez, camels casting long shadows on the glowing sands of the desert en route to El Kabob, and the ultimate romance of Marrakesh.

One of the most memorable events of the tour was the picnic in Ourika, a small village in the High Atlas Mountains, thirty-five miles south of Marrakesh. It was here that each artist discovered his or her favorite painting subject: the uniqueness of the landscape, the mysterious characteristics of the Berber people, or simply the qualities of color and light. And it was here that the artists probably felt most akin to Fortuny, who had dressed as an Arab Moorish countryman in order to inconspicuously

"The Friend," oil on canvas, by Kenneth Riley. Tucson, Arizona, USA. Photo: Sisk
"L'ami," huile sur toile, par Kenneth Riley. Tucson, Arizona, Etats-Unis.

Artistes de l'Ouest américain au Maroc

par Dee Bryers

Le Maroc a enflammé les imaginations des artistes européens longtemps avant le séjour de Matisse à Tanger en 1911 et 1912. Les expressions passionées de Fortuny en 1863, et les oeuvres de Delacroix au début des années 1800 avaient précédé les peintures des odalisques, et de la Marocaine Zorah, de Matisse. De nombreux autres peintres ont aussi représenté le charme et la mystique du Maroc.

Lorsqu'Alf Taylor a invité un groupe peintres de l'Ouest des Etats-Unis, reconnus au niveau national, à faire le tour du Maroc comme ses hôtes en septembre 1984, ils acceptèrent avec un enthousiasme bien naturel. Duane Bryers, Joe Bohler, Nancy Boren, Gerald Fritzler, David Halbach, Tom Hill et Kenneth Riley sont tous des membres d'organisations artistiques prestigieuses, y compris la National Academy of Western Artists (Académie nationale d'Artistes occidentaux), les Cowboy Artists of America (Artistes Cowboy d'Amérique) et la American Watercolor Society (Société américaine d'Aquarelle). Dee Bryers et les artistes Barbara Hill et Marcyne Riley ont accompagné leurs maris dans cette expédition pour faire de la peinture et pour se livrer à des achats.

observe the customs of a culture so foreign to him. Matisse had recalled that "I found the landscapes of Morocco just as they had been described in the paintings of Delacroix." With cameras, brushes and paint, Ourika was recorded on film and canvas, and in the hearts of the artists.

In contrast to the tranquility of the mountainous hinterlands and silent deserts, the raucous activity of the merchants displaying their wares in the claustrophobic labyrinths of the souks presented a palette of colors so flamboyant that they almost discouraged attempts to portray them. The sartorial splendor of the watermen, the veiled and robed figures of Moslem women, and the turbaned vendors were all strong images which demanded pictorial representation, and by which no painter could remain unmoved.

The Islamic art forms, prevalent in every aspect of Moroccan daily life, were noted again and again with exuberant enthusiasm—the vivid patterns of the ceramic mosaics and pottery, the artful mystique and brilliant color compositions of the rugs and textiles, and of course, the intricate craftsmanship of the silver and gold ornamentation. Some of these found their way to Arizona, Texas and Colorado where they were beautifully integrated with American Indian and Mexican crafts in the artists' homes.

The French novelist Flaubert noted while touring North Africa that everything he discovered there, he rediscovered. All of the western artists in the tour group must have felt the same way, as they stuffed their suitcases with sketches, rolls of exposed film, and memories of Morocco.

Dès le moment où les peintres ont aperçu le port de Rabat baigné de soleil doré le soir de leur arrivée, leurs talents créateurs furent stimulés par les vues et les sons excitants du Maroc: les exhibitions éblouissantes d'équitation à la Fantasia de Fez, les chameaux projetant des longues ombres sur le sable embrasé du désert en route à El Kabob, et le charme ultime de Marrakech.

Un des événements les plus mémorables du tour fut le pique-nique à Ourika, un petit village dans le Haut Atlas, cinquante-six kilomètres au sud de Marrakech. C'est ici que chaque peintre a découvert son sujet de peinture favori: le caractère unique du paysage, les traits mystérieux des Berbères, ou tout simplement les qualités particulières de la lumière et des couleurs. Et c'est ici que les artistes ont sans doute mieux compris Fortuny, qui s'était habillé comme un paysan arabe maure pour observer discrètement les coutumes d'une culture qui lui était si étrangère. Matisse s'était souvenu qu'il avait trouvé les paysage du Maroc tout à fait comme ils avaient été décrits dans les peintures de Delacroix. Ourika fut donc enregistré avec des appareils-photo, des pinceaux et de la peinture, sur du filme et du canevas et dans les coeurs des artistes.

En contraste à la tranquilité des arrières-pays mountagneux et des déserts silencieux, l'activité rauque des marchands étalant leurs marchandises dans les labyrinthes claustrophobes des souks présentait une palette de couleurs si flamboyantes qu'elles arrivaient presque à décourager toute tentative de les représenter. La splendeur vestimentaire des vendeurs d'eau, les formes voilées et drapées des femmes musulmanes, les marchands en turbans, tout présentait des images frappantes qui exigeaient d'être peintes et auxquelles aucun peintre ne serait resté insensible.

Les artistes notèrent maintes et maintes fois avec un enthousiasme exubérant les moyens d'expression artistique islamiques, évidents dans tous les aspects de la vie quotidienne au Maroc: les motifs frappants des mosaïques de zelliges et des poteries, la mystique ingénieuse des tapis et textiles et leur composition à couleurs brillantes, et naturellement, le travail superbe et complexe de l'ornementation d'argent et d'or. Quelques-uns de ces trésors furent ramenés en Arizona, au Texas et au Colorado où ils s'accordent à merveille avec les arts des Indiens d'Amérique et du Méxique dans les maisons des artistes.

L'écrivain français Flaubert avait noté, en faisant le tour de l'Afrique du Nord, que tout ce qu'il découvrait là, il redécouvrait. Tous les artistes de l'Ouest dans ce groupe ont sûrement ressenti la même chose en bourrant leurs valises de croquis, de pellicules et de souvenirs du Maroc.

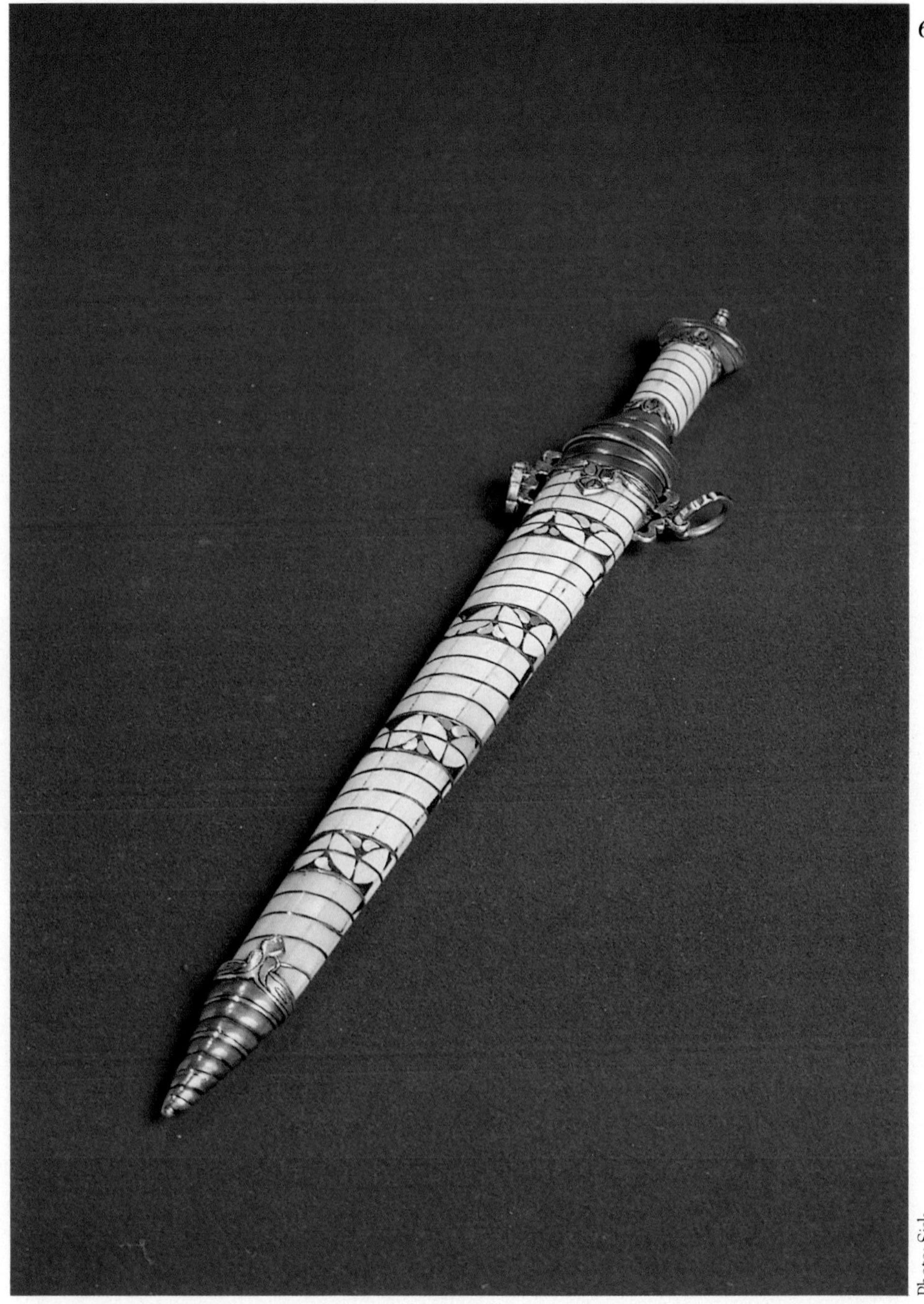

Photo: Sisk

Dagger: Brass, silver and bone. Sahara Desert. AMMA.
Poignard: laiton, argent et os. Désert du Sahara. AMMA.

Photo: Author

Ali of the Sahara and Judi Taylor, dealers of exotic jewelry: Inlaid mirror. AMMA.
Ali du Sahara et Judi Taylor, marchands de bijoux exotiques: miroir incrusté. AMMA.

Photo: Sisk

Inlaid bellows and powder holder: silver, bone, turquoise, coral inlay. McLear Collection.
Soufflet et boîte à poudre, incrustés d'argent, d'os, de turquoise et de corail. Collection de McLear.

Photo: Sisk

Silver chest and box: bone, turquoise and coral inlay. AMMA.
Coffre et boîte en argent, incrustés d'os, de turquoise et de corail. AMMA.

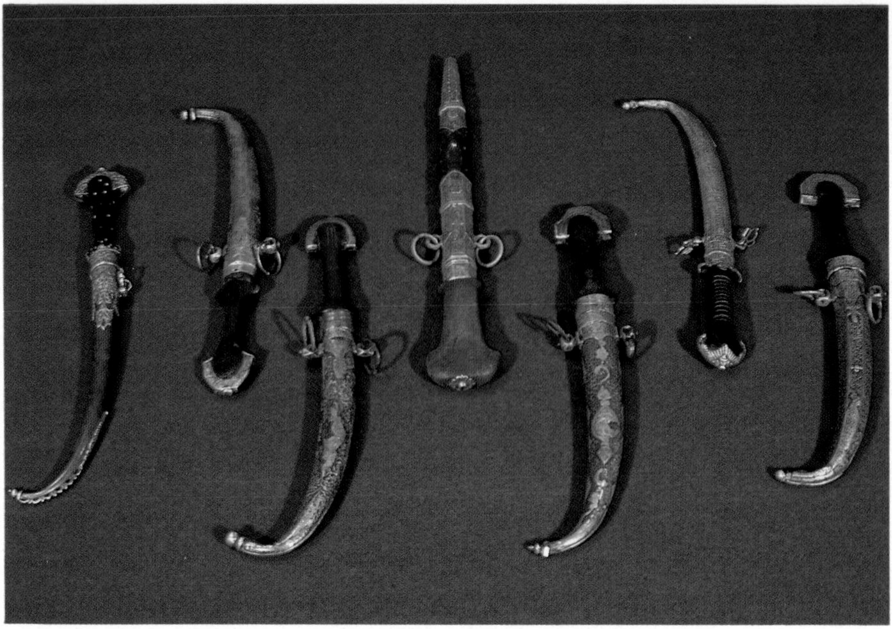

Photo: Sisk

Antique daggers: wood, silver, brass and gold, Sahara Desert. AMMA.
Anciens poignards: bois, argent, laiton et or, désert du Sahara. AMMA.

Photo: Sisk

Antique jewelry and chest: silver, brass, gold, turquoise, coral and amber. AMMA and TMM.
Anciens bijoux et coffre: argent, laiton, or, turquoise, corail et ambre. AMMA et TMM.

Photo: Sisk

Koranic Scriptures embroidered with metallic threads on a piece of tomb cover. AMMA.
Ecritures saintes du Coran brodées en fils métalliques sur un morceau d'ornement de tombeau. AMMA.

Photo: Sisk

Inlaid boxes and Koran holder with rope: bone, silver, turquoise and coral. McLear-Taylor.
Boîtes et coffret avec corde contenant le Coran, incrustés d'os, d'argent, de turquoise et de corail. McLear-Taylor.

Jewelry, Inlay, Etc.

Jewelry and inlay can be found in many styles throughout Morocco, from the delicate gold filigree work of the cities to the heavier coin silver Saharan desert pieces. Silver jewelry is limited and tends to be rather costly: It is often sold by weight. Other metals cost much less. Precious stones are rare, but coral, amber, turquoise and colored stones are used frequently. Reproductions are abundant and beautiful, and imitation coins and amber are used on less expensive jewelry.

Look at these photos: All of this is real, and made in Morocco!

Les bijoux, l'incrustation, etc.

On retrouve plusieurs styles de bijoux et d'incrustation à travers le Maroc, du filigrane en or délicat des villes aux bijoux plus lourds fabriqués de pièces d'argent dans le désert du Sahara. La bijouterie en argent est peu abondante et tend à coûter assez cher: elle se vend souvent au poids. D'autres métaux sont beaucoup meilleur marché. Les pierres précieuses sont rares, mais on trouve souvent du corail, de l'ambre, du turquoise et des pierres fines. Les reproductions sont abondantes et belles, et les orfèvres utilisent des fausses pièces de monnaie et de l'ambre artificiel pour fabriquer les bijoux moins chers.

Regardez ces photos: tout ceci est véritable et fabriqué au Maroc!

Gold and silver antique flintlock and sword, silk belts, brass trays. AMMA. *Photo: Sisk*
Ancien fusil à baguettes et ancienne épée en or et argent, ceintures en soie, plateaux en laiton. AMMA.

Photo: Sisk

To the Treasure Hunters of the World

Aux chasseurs de trésors du monde

Bronze of a boy on a carpet, by Bergman, 18th Century, Austria. AMMA.
Bronze d'un garçon couché sur un tapis, par Bergman, 18ème siècle, Autriche. AMMA.

Photo: Sisk

Yesterday...
Hier...

"Moroccan Rug Merchant," oil, circa 1902. AMMA.
"Marchand de tapis marocain," huile, circa 1902. AMMA.

Photo: J. Taylor

Today. . .
aujourd'hui...

The author and Noureddine examine old pottery from the Sahara.
L'auteur et Noureddine examinent de la vieille céramique du Sahara.

and Tomorrow

et demain

Children's rug with expectant camels. Gregory Michael Ussery Collection. Photo: Author
Petit tapis d'enfants représentant des chamelles enceintes. Collection de Gregory Michael Ussery.

Photo: Author

Gregory Michael Ussery: Libra, October 7, 1989. Villa America, Rabat, Morocco.
Gregory Michael Ussery: balance, 7 octobre 1989. Villa America, Rabat, Maroc.

Photo: Hampton

Dye market, Marrakesh.
Marché de teintures, Marrakech.

Resplendent Diversity: Carpets and Textiles of Morocco

by Claire Campbell Park

Contemporary and traditional, urban and rural, from rich brocades and embroideries to flatweaves and pile rugs full of color and character, the textiles of Morocco reflect the diversity of the country and its people.

This exhibition focuses on textiles from the three major cultural traditions of Morocco: Berber, Rural Arab, and Urban Arab. The selections for the exhibition were made from the collection of Alf Taylor's American Museum of Moroccan Art, the most comprehensive collection in the United States. Because of the comprehensive nature of the collection, this exhibition is the first to display Moroccan textiles by tribe or city of origin. The Taylor Collection commemorates the 1787 signing of the Treaty of Amity with Morocco—the longest unbroken treaty in U.S. history. Resplendent Diversity, held at the Old Pueblo Museum, was curated by Claire Campbell Park (See Pp.72-5,80-4,91,93-6,100).

Diversité resplendissante: tapis et textiles du Maroc

Contemporains et traditionnels, urbains et ruraux, des riches brocards et broderies aux tapis à poil ras et à haute laine pleins de couleurs et de caractère, les textiles du Maroc reflètent la diversité du pays et de populations.

Cette exposition se concentre sur les textiles des trois principales traditions culturelles du Maroc: berbère, arabe rurale, et arabe urbaine. Les sélections pour l'exposition proviennent de la collection du Musée américain d'Art marocain d'Alf Taylor, la collection la plus vaste des Etats-Unis. C'est l'étendue de cette collection qui a permis qu'on expose pour la première fois des textiles marocains par tribu ou ville d'origine. La Collection Taylor commémore la signature du Traité d'Amitié avec le Maroc de 1787—le traité tenu le plus longtemps dans l'histoire de Etats-Unis. Diversité resplendissante, Old Pueblo Museum, était conçue par Claire Campbell Park *(Voir Pp.72-5,80-4,91,93-6,100)*.

Photo: Sisk

Resplendent Diversity: Carpets and Textiles of Morocco. Old Pueblo Museum, Tucson, AZ, USA.
Diversité resplendissante: tapis et textiles du Maroc. Old Pueblo Museum, Tucson, AZ, Etats-Unis.

Photos: Sisk

Berber

The Berbers are a pastoral people and have inhabited Morocco since long before the first Arabs arrived in the 7th Century A.D. Although they have adopted the Arab's religion of Islam, their culture remains distinct. This saddle blanket is from the Zemmour tribe of the Middle Atlas Mountains. The Middle Atlas Berbers are known for their masterful use of the complementary weft technique used in the patterned areas of this blanket. The Berbers of the High Atlas Mountains weave colorful pile rugs and optically striped shawls.

Textiles berbères

Les Berbères sont un peuple pastoral qui a habité le Maroc longtemps avant l'arrivée des premiers Arabes au huitième siècle de notre ère. Malgré le fait que les Berbères ont adopté la religion islamique des Arabes, leur culture reste différente de celle de ces derniers. Ce tapis de selle provient de la tribu Zemmour du Moyen Atlas. Les Berbères du Moyen Atlas sont connus pour leur maîtrise de la technique de trames complémentaires utilisée dans les parties de ce tapis ornées de motifs. Les Berbères du Haut Atlas tissent des tapis colorés à haute laine et des châles rayés à effets optiques.

Berber/Middle Atlas/Zemmour

The Zemmour have gradually moved northwest from the Sahara Desert through the centuries to their present location. They have occupied the present area on the plains between Rabat and Meknes for one hundred years. This semi-nomadic lifestyle of frequent uprooting in search of good pasture land for their flocks is known as transhumance.

The Zemmour are well-known for their weaving and remain among the most prolific weavers of modern Morocco. An identifying characteristic of their weaving is the red ground punctuated by bands of colorful and intricate complementary weft technique patterning.

Berbère/Moyen Atlas/Zemmour

Les Zemmour s'étaient graduellement dirigés vers le nord-ouest du désert du Sahara aux cours des siècles pour s'établir dans leur emplacement actuel. Ils occupent cette région dans les plaines entre Rabat et Meknès depuis cent ans. Ce mode de vie semi-nomade avec le déracinement fréquent à la recherche de bons pâturages pour leurs troupeaux s'appelle la transhumance.

Les Zemmour sont connus pour leur tissage, et ils font toujours partie des tisserands les plus prolifiques du Maroc contemporain. Un fond rouge ponctué de bandes de motifs colorés compliqués de trames complémentaires est une caractéristique de leur tissage qui les identifie.

Saddle Blankets and Saddle Bags (Tayttait and Ssmatt)

Consistently the most exquisitely woven and elaborately designed items woven by the Zemmour are the saddle blankets and saddle bags used by the men in the Fantasia, the ceremonial games of horsemanship performed at many Berber festivals. These are items of great prestige and honor which can also be displayed during the weekly visit to the local market (souk). The blankets are draped over the saddle, not under it. The saddle bags hang over the back of the saddle and are used to carry gunpowder and personal gear.

Tapis de selle et sacoches (Tayttait et Ssmatt)

Les articles toujours tissés de façon la plus exquise et conçus de façon la plus élaborée par les Zemmour sont les tapis de selle et les sacoches utilisés par les hommes dans les Fantasias, les jeux d'équitation cérémoniels joués à beaucoup de festivals berbères. Ces articles rapportent beaucoup de prestige et d'honneur à leurs propriétaires, et ceux-ci peuvent aussi les exhiber pendant leurs visites hebdomadaires au marché local (souk). Les selles sont recouvertes des tapis au lieu de reposer sur eux. Les sacoches sont drapées sur l'arriière de la selle et contiennent de la poudre à canon et des équipements personnels.

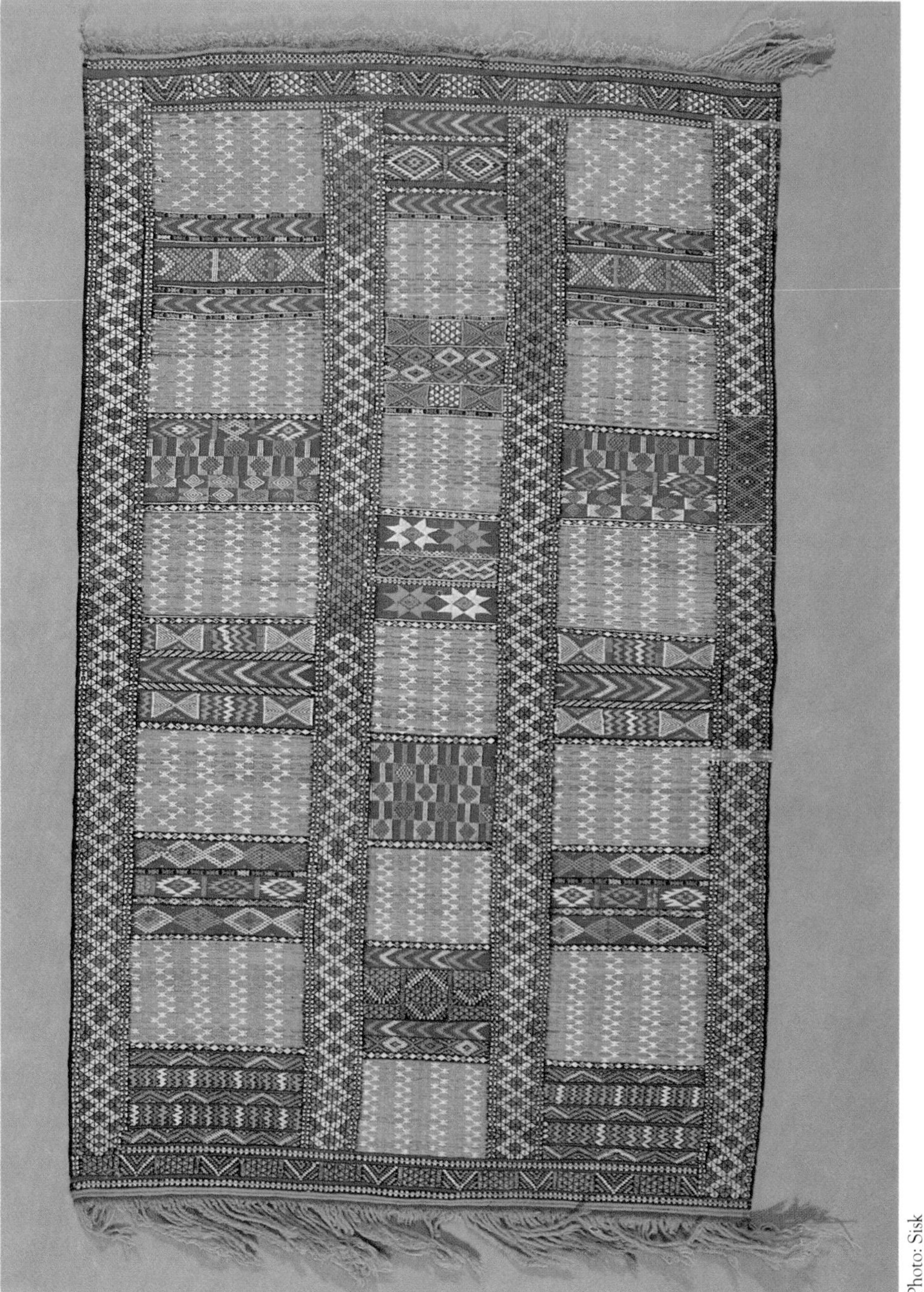

Photo: Sisk

Zemmour Berber saddle rug (flatweave) c. 1910: Wool, cotton and silk. AMMA.
Tapis de selle berbère zemmour (tissage à poil ras) c. 1910: laine, coton et soie. AMMA.

Photo: Sisk

Middle Atlas Berber cushion and saddle bag, early 20th Century. AMMA.
Coussin et sacoche de selle berbères du Moyen Atlas, début du 20ème siècle. AMMA.

Photo: Author

Loom for weaving belts and small bags. Museum of the Oudaias, Rabat.
Métier à tisser pour ceintures et petits sacs. Musée des Oudaias, Rabat.

Photo: Walker

Mouda: A Zemmour Berber weaver at her loom. Tiflet.
Mouda: une tisseuse berbère à son métier. Tiflet.

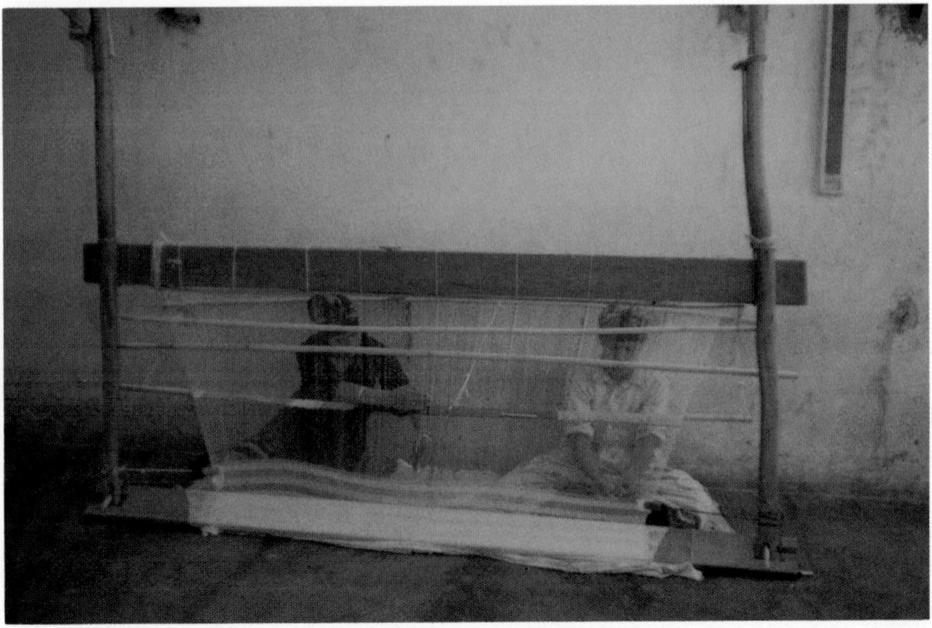

Photo: Hahn

Weavers of Bzou: wool and silk fabric woven for royalty for 400 years.
Tisseuses de Bzou: tissus de laine et de soie tissés pour la famille royalle depuis 400 ans.

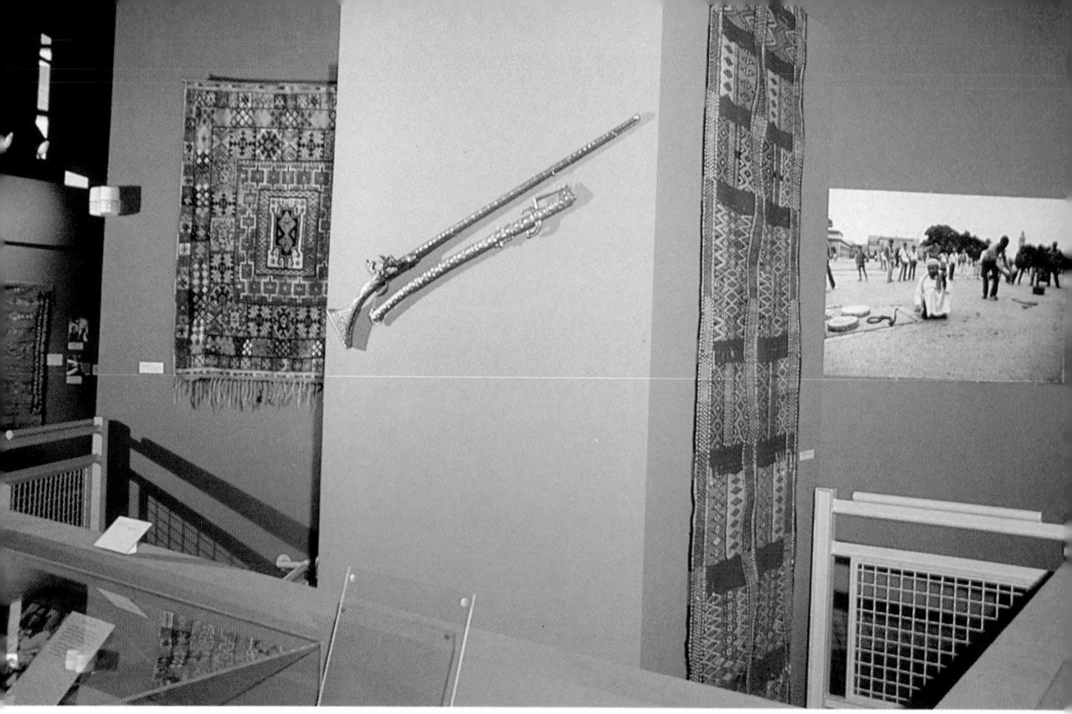

Photos: Sisk

Photo: Sisk

"Moroccan Tents," watercolor by Joseph Bohler, Colorado.
"Tentes marocaines," aquarelle de Joseph Bohler, Colorado.

Photo: Sisk

Above: Sultan's ceremonial tent. OPM. *Tente cérémonielle d'un sultan*. OPM.
Opposite: Tent band, gold and silver weapons. OPM. *Bande pour une tente, armes en or et argent*. OPM.
Zemmour tent with Moroccan textiles. OPM. *Tente zemmour avec textiles marocaines*. OPM.
Photo: Sisk

Photo: Sisk

Berber/Middle Atlas/Beni M'Guild

The Beni M'Guild are a pastoral people who have gradually moved from the Sahara to their present location in the Middle Atlas Mountains. Although they live in close proximity to the Zemmour, characteristics that distinguish their weaving from the Zemmour's include: 1) The complementary weft techniques which nearly cover the surface of most weavings, rather than being used in bands separated by plain weave (exceptions are the man's blanket and tent bands); 2) the minimal use of red, which is replaced by an abundance of blue and darker colors.

Berbères/Moyen Atlas/Beni M'Guild

Les Beni M'Guild sont un peuple pastoral qui est graduellement venu du Sahara pour s'établir dans son emplacement actuel dans le Moyen Atlas. Bien qu'ils habitent tout près des Zemmour, plusieurs caractéristiques distinguent leur tissage de celui des Zemmour, à savoir: 1) les techniques de trames complémentaires qui couvrent presque toute la surface de la plupart de leurs textiles, au lieu d'être utilisées en bandes séparées par de la toile (les couvertures des hommes et les bandes des tentes sont des exceptions); 2) L'usage minimal du rouge, remplacé par une abondance de bleu et de couleurs plus foncées.

Zemmour Tent

The tent (axam) (p. 80) was once the main dwelling of the Zemmour but is now more often a supplement to a house. However, many rural families still live in a tent during the summer when they move their flocks to higher pasture. The tent is the only item woven on a long horizontal ground loom, rather than a vertical loom. It consists of long bands woven of wool and goat hair that are dyed black and then sewn together.

Tente des Zemmour

La tente (axam) était autrefois l'habitation principale des Zemmour, mais actuellement elle est plus souvent un supplément à la maison. Cependant, beaucoup de familles rurales habitent toujours dans des tentes pendant l'été quand elles font paître leurs troupeaux dans les pâturages plus élevés. La tente est le seul article tissé sur le long métier horizontal au lieu du métier vertical. Elle consiste en de longues bandes en laine et poil de chèvre tissées, teintes en noir et cousues ensemble.

Berber/High Atlas
Ait Ouaouzguite - Non-traditional

During the French Protectorate (1912-1956), the French established a weaving workshop, or atelier, in the Town of Tazenakht in the Ait Ouaouzguite region. This atelier was strictly for pile rugs (p. 84) and the directors instructed their weavers to alter the traditional designs in ways they felt would be more marketable in Europe. This influence has led to all manner of interesting deviations from tradition in the pile rugs from the Tazenakht area.

Berbère/Haut Atlas
Ait Ouaouzguite - non-traditionnel

Pendant le protectorat français (1912-1956), les Français établirent un atelier de tissage dans la ville de Tazenakht, située dans la région de Ait Ouaouzguite. C'était un atelier strictement pour les tapis à haute laine, et les directeurs avaient chargé les tisserandes d'altérer les motifs traditionnels de manière à les rendre plus facilement vendables en Europe, selon les opinions de ces premiers. Cette influence a mené à toutes sortes de déviations intéressantes des traditions des tapis à haute laine de la région de Tazenakht.

Photo: Sisk

Rug honoring the Green March, Nov. 6, 1975, High Atlas, wool, non-traditional. OPM.
Tapis honorant la Marche Verte, 6 nov. 1975, Haut Atlas, laine, non-traditionnel. OPM.

Photo: Sisk

High Atlas rug, traditional, Glaoua Tribe, wool, 19th Century. AMMA.
Tapis du Haut Atlas, traditionnel, tribu Glaoua, laine, 19ème siècle. AMMA.

Photo: Hahn

High Atlas Berber cape: Wool and silk, 19th Century. AMMA.
Cape berbère du Haut Atlas: laine et soie, 19ème siècle. AMMA.

Tribal Capes and Ceremonial Blankets

by Jerry Whitney

I live in the Southwest and have always loved and collected tribal art, so when I met Alf Taylor and had a chance to see his Moroccan weavings, I was intrigued. As fate would have it, I was offered, and accepted, an invitation to join the privileged handful of people who have accompanied Alf to Morocco. The experience was unforgettable.

Morocco is a beautiful, serene country, and the people have a calm, proud quality reflecting a culture that has been successful through centuries of history. Making useful and beautiful weavings from their excellent wool was, and still is, an important part of this success.

Marrakesh is the trade center of Morocco, and that is where I fell in love with the country and with the Moroccan and Berber weaving arts. Before we entered the souks, Alf gave me a few important tips: to jump to one side when I hear "BALEK!" ("Move aside!") behind me; not to be afraid to ask to see something from the bottom of the stack; and to be prepared to buy from the heart. So the fun begins!

The souks are a maze of narrow alleys with shops and stands in profusion, and in no apparent order. First we went through the spice market, then through the garment, copper and brass, and jewelry markets, each one rich in exotic wonders never found in a mall. The rug market was the most magical of all, and as we penetrated its shady depths, Alf's friends greeted us and sent for mint tea.

Sipping tea and exchanging pleasantries merely whetted my appetite for seeing some of the pieces which were folded and stacked against the shop walls. Finally, wool would delicately enter the conversation and a piece would be carefully selected to be shown to us. We could spend the afternoon looking at three pieces or three hundred. The merchants seem serenely unperturbed either way. As we looked at a variety of rugs, tent wall hangings, capes, cushions, blankets and saddlebags, I began to realize that, to me, nothing is as interesting as the weavings which have been designed and woven to wear.

There are many tribes in North Africa, and each tribe produces a distinctive blanket. Available dyes and social customs, as well as geography, are the causes of the wide variety in styles. The colors, shape and design identifies the tribe which the wearer belongs to. If the cape is woven especially evenly, the wool is shiny and soft, and the colors are deep and vibrant, the wearer garners an extra measure of respect. The women are the weavers in Berber culture, and everyone has sheep and wool. Understandably, turning the wool into one of the refinements of life is a matter of great importance and pride. Mothers teach their daughters carefully, as their chances for marrying well increase with their weaving skill. The tribal cape is the most visible tribute to the weaver's art, so while most pieces which come to market have been worn, their apparent beauty is only enhanced by having a personal history.

The tribal names of the weavings spin in my head. I am dazzled by a white fringed blanket with crossing lines of sparkling sequins. I'm told it's a Zaiane Snow Cape. Zaiane, as well as all tribal names, describes a people who were nomadic in the past. Although there were preferences as far as elevation is concerned, no specific region could be identified with the tribe living there, for the tribes were just passing through. The ones who traveled in the higher elevations wove more weatherproof capes. The Beni Ouarain left long loops of wool hanging in profusion on one side of the blankets they wore. In inclement weather, the snow and water would hit the loops and drip off, rather than soaking through. Clothed in richly decorated textiles with alternative stripes of deep reds and browns in complex tribal symbols, these people knew how to dress to impress. Simple but serious capes from one high Atlas tribe in solid black and red contrasted with the complex patterns favored by the Ait Haddidou tribe. Well, I finally hyperventilated and had to be led away, and this was only the first of many shops to be visited that day.

Following my first introduction to Morocco, I now visit and shop the souks of Marrakesh each time I go there, but I also love to explore other parts of the country. I've learned that excellent weavings are where you find them, and the villages and country markets are sources of treasures as well as adventures.

Since I am a traveler as well as a collector, my home reflects my love of folk and tribal art, but nothing has made as much of an impact on my decor as the Berber capes and blankets. Knowing something about the woman who wove and wore the black and white striped Ait Haddidou cape that hangs on my living room wall deepens my appreciation and love for the piece. Atlas Berber girls, such as the one who previously wore my cape, marry a man chosen by their parents by the age fifteen or sixteen. If the marriage doesn't work out, the newlywed couple parts and returns to their parents' homes, sometimes as soon as two or three weeks later. No judgement is passed and they are then free to choose their own mates. These same Ait Haddidou people, one of more than two hundred different Berber tribes of Morocco, have a bridal fair where bachelors and unmarried or divorced daughters meet in an ancient custom where instant courtship, engagements, and marriage vows take place amid the regional trade market and the celebration of a local saint's day (*National Geographic Magazine*, June 1968 and January 1980). When the woman accepts her suitor's request for her hand in marriage, she tells him that he has captured her liver. The liver, not the heart, is considered the center of love.

The knowledge that each tribal piece has an interesting story as well as beauty and value keeps calling me back to Morocco to seek new treasures, adventures and information. My love affair with Morocco intensifies with each visit.

Capes et couvertures cérémonielles tribales

par Jerry Whitney

J'habite au sud-ouest des Etats-Unis et j'ai toujours aimé et collectionné les arts tribaux; j'étais donc très intriguée quand j'ai rencontré Alf Taylor et que j'ai eu l'occasion de voir ses textiles marocains. Comme le sort l'a décidé, on m'a invitée à me joindre au petit groupe privilégié qui a accompagné Alf au Maroc, et j'ai accepté. L'expérience fut inoubliable.

Le Maroc est un beau pays serein et son peuple possède des qualités de calme et de fierté qui reflètent une culture marquée de succès durant des siècles d'histoire. La fabrication de ses beaux textiles utilitaires de sa laine excellente a joué, et joue toujours, un rôle important dans son succès.

Marrakech est le centre commercial du Maroc et c'est là où je me suis éprise d'amour pour ce pays et pour les arts de tissage marocains et berbères. Avant d'entrer dans les souks, Alf m'a donné quelques conseils importants: de m'écarter vite quand j'entends "BALEK!" ("écartez-vous!") derrière moi; de ne pas hésiter à demander de voir quelque chose au bas de la pile; et d'être prête à faire des achats du fond du coeur. Et voilà, on commence à s'amuser!

Les souks sont un labyrinthe d'allées étroites avec une profusion de magasins et d'étalages sans organisation apparente. Nous allons d'abord au marché d'épices, et ensuite nous traverserons les marchés d'habits, de cuivre et de laiton, et de bijoux, chacun riche en merveilles exotiques qu'on ne trouve jamais dans les allées commerciales chez nous. Le marché de tapis est le plus magique de tous, et comme nous pénétrons ses profondeurs ombragées, les amis d'Alf nous saluent et envoyent chercher du thé à la menthe.

Boire du thé et échanger des civilités, cela stimule tout simplement mon désir de voir quelques-unes des pièces pliées et entassées contre les murs des magasins. Finalement, la laine entre délicatement dans la conversation et on choisit une pièce avec soin pour nous la montrer. Nous pouvons passer l'après-midi à regarder trois pièces ou trois cent. Le marchand semble sereinement tranquille quoi qu'il arrive. En regardant toute une diversité de tapis, de tapisseries pour les tentes, de capes et de coussins, de couvertures et de sacoches de selle, je commence à constater qu'il n'y a rien de plus intéressant que les textiles qu'on a conçus et tissés comme vêtements.

Il y a plusieurs tribus en Afrique du Nord, et chacune produit sa propre couverture caractéristique. Les teintures disponibles et les coutumes sociales sont les causes d'une grande diversité de styles, tout autant que la géographie. Les couleurs, formes et motifs identifient la tribu à laquelle appartient la personne qui les porte. Si la cape est tissée de façon particulièrement fine, si la laine est lustrée et moelleuse, et si les couleurs sont vives et vibrantes, la personne qui les porte gagne du respect supplémentaire. C'est les femmes qui font le tissage dans la culture berbère, et tout le monde a des moutons et de la laine. Naturellement, la transformation de la laine en un des raffimenents de la vie est une affaire de grande importance et une source de fierté. Les mères l'enseignent soigneusement à leurs filles, puisque les chances de ces dernières de faire un bon mariage augmentent en mesure de leurs techniques de tissage. La cape tribale est l'hommage le plus visible à l'art de la tisserande; ainsi, comme on a déjà porté la plupart des pièces qui viennent sur le marché, leur beauté apparente est simplement rehaussée par le fait qu'elles ont une histoire personnelle.

Les noms tribaux des textiles tournent dans ma tête. Une couverture blanche à franges avec des lignes de paillettes étincelantes qui s'entrecroisent m'éblouit. On me dit que c'est une cape Zaiane pour la neige. Le nom Zaiane, comme tous les noms des tribus, décrit un peuple qui était nomade autrefois. Bien qu'il y ait parmi les tribus des préférences en ce qui concerne l'altitude, on ne peut identifier aucune région spécifique avec une tribu particulière, car ces dernières ne restaient pas en place. Les tribus qui fréquentaient les plus hautes altitudes tissaient des capes plus imperméables. Les Beni Ouarain laissaient des longues boucles de laine pendre en profusion d'un côté des couvertures qu'ils portaient. Quand le temps était inclément, la neige

Photo: Hahn

Young girl of the Middle Atlas Mountains in her green sequinned blanket.
Jeune fille du Moyen Atlas dans sa couverture verte à paillettes.

Photo: Bertrand, Marrakesh

Woman of the Ait Haddidou Tribe: Bridal Festival of Imillchil.
Femme de la tribu Ait Haddidou: festival nuptial d'Imillchil.

Photo: Sisk

Tribes are distinguished by the color of their blankets: High Atlas Mountains. OPM.
Les tribus se distinguent par la couleur de leurs couvertures: Haut Atlas. OPM.

et la pluie tombaient sur les boucles et en dégouttaient, au lieu de tremper les couvertures. Ces gens, habillés richement en rayures alternantes de rouges et marrons vifs formant des symboles tribaux complexes, savaient comment s'habiller pour impressionner les autres. Les capes simples mais sérieuses en rouge et noir unis d'une des tribus du Haut Atlas contrastent avec les motifs complexes favorisés par la tribu Ait Haddidou. Enfin, j'ai commencé à perdre haleine et on a dû m'emmener, mais ce n'était que le premier des nombreux magasins à visiter ce jour-là.

Depuis cette première introduction au Maroc, je visite et fais des achats aux souks de Marrakech chaque fois que j'y vais, mais j'aime aussi explorer d'autres parties du pays. J'ai appris que les textiles excellents sont là où on les trouve, et les marchés des villages et de la campagne sont des sources de trésors aussi bien que d'aventures.

Puisque je suis voyageuse aussi bien que collectionneuse, ma maison reflète mon amour des arts folkloriques et tribaux, mais de tous mes objets d'art, les capes et couvertures berbères ont eu le plus d'impact sur mon décor. Le fait que je sais quelque chose au sujet de la femme qui a tissé et porté la cape Ait Haddidou rayée de noir et blanc suspendue au mur de mon salon approfondit mon appréciation de ce vêtement et ma passion pour lui. Les filles berbères de l'Atlas, comme celle qui avait porté ma cape, marient un homme choisi par leurs parents dès l'âge de quinze ou de seize ans. Si cette union ne réussit pas, les jeunes mariés se séparent et retournent chez leurs parents, parfois après deux ou trois semaines seulement. Aucun jugement n'est prononcé et ils sont maintenant libres de choisir leurs propres époux. Les Ait Haddidou, une des plus de deux cent tribus berbères du Maroc, a une foire matrimoniale où les célibataires hommes et femmes et les divorcés se rencontrent selon une ancienne coutume où on se fait la cour, on se fiance et on se marie sur-le-champ au milieu du marché commercial régional et de la célébration du jour de fête d'un saint local (National Geographic Magazine, *juin 1968 et janvier 1980). Quand la femme accepte le propos de mariage de son soupirant, elle lui dit qu'il a gagné son foie. C'est le foie, et non pas le coeur, que ces gens considèrent comme le siège de l'amour.*

La conviction que chaque pièce tribale a une histoire intéressante aussi bien que de la beauté et de la valeur me rappelle constamment au Maroc à la recherche de nouveaux trésors, de nouvelles aventures et de nouvelles connaissances. Mon amour pour le Maroc s'approfondit avec chaque visite.

Photo: Bertrand, Marrakesh

Berbers of the Middle Atlas Mountains, Zaiane Tribe.
Berbères des montagnes du Moyen Atlas, tribu Zaiane.

Photo: Sisk

Snow capes of the Middle Atlas Mountains, Beni Ouarain Tribe. OPM.
Capes pour la neige des montagnes du Moyen Atlas, tribu Beni Ouarain. OPM.

Rugs of the rural Arabs. OPM. Photo: Sisk. *Tapis des Arabes ruraux. OPM.*

Rural Arab

The rural Arab tribes of the Tennsift River region were originally nomadic. They were brought to Morocco to fight wars for ruling Arab groups and were then rewarded with land. Their weaving is characteristically free-spirited in design and suggests the concept of individual expression rather than the restraining influences of a long weaving tradition. This pile rug is from the Rehamna tribe.

Arabes ruraux

Les tribus arabes rurales de la région du fleuve Tennsift étaient nomades à l'origine. Les groupes arabes qui dominaient la région les ont amenés au Maroc comme mercenaires et les ont ensuite récompensés avec des dons de terre. La composition de leur tissage manifeste typiquement un esprit de liberté qui suggère le concepte d'expression individuelle plutôt que les influences limitantes d'une longue tradition de tissage. Ce tapis à haute laine provient de la tribu Rehamna.

Rural Arab – Tennsift River Region

The rural Arab tribes of the Tennsift River region include the Oulad-Bousbaa, Chiadma, Ahmar, and Rehamna.

Since very early in their history, the weaving of the Rural Arabs has displayed a degree of freedom of design that seems closer to the concept of individual expression than the restraining influence of group tradition. An exception to this pronounced originality was a period during which weavers were strongly influenced by Rabat carpets; this period reached its peak during the last half of the 19th Century.

Arabes ruraux – Région du fleuve Tennsift

Les tribus arabes rurales de la région du fleuve Tennsift comprennent les Oulad-Bousbaa, Chiadma, Ahmar, and Rehamna.

Rural Arab rug, Rehamna Tribe, wool, 7'x8', mid 20th Century. OPM. Photo Sisk
Tapis arabe rural, tribu Rehamna, laine, milieu du 20ème siècle. OPM.

Depuis les périodes précoces de leur histoire, le tissage des Arabes ruraux a montré un degré de liberté de conception qui rappelle le concepte d'expression individuelle plutôt que les influences conservatrices d'une longue tradition de tissage. Une exception à cette originalité marquée a apparu durant la période où les tisserandes étaient fortement influencées par les tapis de Rabat; cette période a atteint son apogée pendant la dernière moitié du dix-neuvième siècle.

The author watches an urban Arab weaver. Ensemble Artisanal, Rabat. Photo: Hahn
L'auteur regarde une tisseuse arabe urbaine. Ensemble Artisanal, Rabat.

Urban Arab/Rabat

Rabat is the present-day capital of Morocco. Rabat rugs began to be made during the 18th Century, when maritime travel to Mecca became much more feasible and the urban Arab textile tradition of Asia Minor became more accessible. This tradition is characterized by floral motifs, central medallions, and borders. The Rabat rugs are woven by professional weavers in urban workshops for the upper class.

Rabat rugs have had a strong influence on the pile rugs of both the Berber and Rural Arab tribes, who became familiar with the rugs through their privileged members. Pilgrims to Mecca would return with urban Islamic pile rugs they had purchased in Rabat or elsewhere. When caids and notables from the rural regions were called to court, they would often return with Rabat rugs.

Rabat rugs have long been associated with prestige and royalty, and were frequently given as presents of influence. Even today, Moroccan merchants sometimes use the term "the King's rugs" when displaying Rabat carpets.

Arabes urbains/Rabat

Rabat est la capitale actuelle du Maroc. On a commencé à fabriquer les tapis de Rabat au dix-huitième siècle, quand les voyages à la Mecque en bateau sont devenus beaucoup plus faciles et la tradition textile des Arabes urbains de l'Asie Mineure est devenue plus accessible. Cette tradition est caractérisée par des motifs floraux, des médallions centraux et des listels. Les tapis de Rabat sont tissés par des tisserandes professionelles dans des ateliers urbains, pour des clients de niveau social élevé.

Photo: Hahn

Urban Arab rug, wool, Rabat, 18th Century. Musée national de l'Artisanat, Rabat.
Tapis arabe urbain, laine, Rabat, 18ème siècle. Musée national de l'Artisanat, Rabat.

Les tapis de Rabat ont beaucoup influencé les tapis à haute laine des tribus berbères et d'Arabes ruraux, qui se sont familiarisées avec ces tapis grâce à leurs membres privilégiés. Les pèlerins de la Mecque revenaient avec des tapis islamiques urbains à haute laine qu'ils avaient achetés à Rabat ou ailleurs. Quand les caïds et notables des régions rurales étaient mandés à la cour, ils revenaient souvent avec des tapis de Rabat.

Les tapis de Rabat ont été associés avec le prestige et la royauté depuis longtemps, et on les donnait souvent comme cadeaux d'influence. Même aujourd'hui, les marchands marocains utilisent parfois le terme "tapis du Roi" quand ils exhibent les tapis de Rabat.

Photo: Sisk

Urban Arab rug, Rabat, 19th Century. OPM.
Tapis arabe urbain, Rabat, 19ème siècle. OPM.

Photo: Sisk

Urban Arab rug, wool, Rabat, 7' x 14', 19th Century. OPM.
Tapis arabe urbain, laine, Rabat, 19ème siècle. OPM.

Photo: Sisk

A haiti placed against a wall facing Mecca for praying, 6' x 20', Mid 20th Century. OPM.
Haiti placé contre un mur face à la Mecque pour les prières, milieu du 20ème siècle. OPM.

Photo: Sisk

Hand embroidered silk on silk curtain, mid 20th Century. Silk wedding belts, Fez. OPM.
Rideau de soie brodé de soie à la main, milieu du 20ème siècle. Ceintures de mariée en soie, Fès. OPM.

Photo: Author

Silk wedding belt showing pattern change, Fez. AMMA.
Céinture de mariée avec changement de motifs, Fès. AMMA.

EMBROIDERY

The embroideries of Morocco eloquently speak to the human desire for articles of beauty in an everyday setting. Created primarily in the cities of Rabat, Sale, Meknes, Fez, Tetouan, Chichaoua, and Azemmour, embroidery in Morocco is an urban phenomenon reflecting the complex ebb and flow of Islamic and non-Islamic peoples, and influences from Andalusia, the Mediterranean, and other regions of North Africa. Refugees from the Christian reconquest of Spain, the Portuguese conquest of portions of the Moroccan coastline, the pressure of Turkish expansion from the east, and French colonial occupation each influenced the character and practice of embroidery in Morocco during the last 4 to 5 centuries. Many of the external influences in motifs and techniques transmitted as part of this history had antecedents in the Classical and Byzantine periods. Surviving examples, however, represent only the 18th through the 20th centuries. In the same regions, the indigenous Berber population maintained a separate and distinct weaving tradition.

Women of both Arab and Jewish communities embellished household textiles and apparel with silk and metallic thread embroidery. Embroidery designs were used to decorate soft furnishings such as cushion and mattress covers, curtains, wall and door hangings, shawls, head scarves, bath veils, tray covers, and handkerchiefs. Embroidery motifs on these items were created using untwisted silk floss on a plain weave cotton or linen ground fabric. Very fine sashes or handkerchiefs utilized silk background fabric. Particular colors and stitch selections characterized each city. For example, Chichaoua embroideries are multicolored with geometric repeats organized in panels of design, while early Rabat embroideries are often in a monochromatic blue, red, or purple dense floral pattern. Fez embroidery designs are structured by a reversible counted thread technique which incorporates the ground fabric as a grid for the completed needlework. Azemmour embroideries reflect Renaissance Italian and Spanish patterns in that the design is created by the negative image left after covering the background with counted stitches (as in Asissi work). Motif choices include chimera, griffins, birds flanking a central vase, and stylized women with upraised arms and full triangular skirts. In Rabat and Tetouan, designs may be first drawn free hand and then filled with stitches. Satin stitch, stem stitch, long-armed cross stitch, darning stitch, and double-sided marking cross stitch are the most prevalent. A Turkish-type embroidery frame was used in areas such as Fez, while in other regions the Spanish method of pinning the fabric to a tightly stuffed cushion held on the knees was employed.

Particularly fine and elaborate gold thread embroidery for clothing was produced by the Jewish needleworkers of Tetouan. The marriage costume of bolero vest, wide belt, and wrap-around skirt was emblazoned with ornate buttons and gold embroidery as part of the bride's dowry. Fez is another renowned gold embroidery center. Gold and silver embroidery is usually couched on velvet or leather and is most often found on belts, pillows, koran covers, shoes, and hats. Other gold-embroidered articles include the "haiti" or wall coverings used both in houses and tents, designed as a series of connecting arch motifs either embroidered in gold on velvet or constructed by an applique technique (illus. p. 100).

Women execute the embroidery. Men finish the construction of pouches, slippers, and headwear. Saddle embroidery, for which Fez is famous, is especially difficult, and is undertaken by men, while the saddle cloth and cover is decorated by women. Both men and women participate in making braids, tassels and trimmings. Such embellishments may be added as finishing to the ornate brocade fabrics woven with silk and metal threads for belts, women's caftans, and upholstery (illus. p. 100, 101). Men in the workshops create complex patterns on jacquard looms from traditional Moroccan motifs, Islamic-Andalusian derived designs and European influences. Belts of this type combine four or more patterns, usually in alternating geometric and floral designs. As these are worn folded in half lengthwise and wrapped around the waist, the wearer could change the belt by simply wrapping in a different direction or by reversing sides. Ground fabrics such as these could receive additional embroidery embellishment.

Young women were taught to embroider as apprentices to a master embroideress, or ma'allema. This individual provided instruction for payment or gifts and might be a family member or friend. As in other parts of the world, the students produced samplers to demonstrate mastery of techniques and as pattern and stitch reminders. Unlike European and American counterparts, however, they rarely included calligraphic examples. The skilled ma'allema could be commissioned to create free-form designs or to execute a particular finished product, although most Moroccan women created embroideries for personal use.

As in other domestic-based arts, personal creativity, preference, and technical excellence all found expression through the individual Moroccan embroiderer. In contrast to the plain exterior household facade separating the family from the outer world, a woman's needlework furnished a vibrant and colorful inner world with meaning and tradition defined through her handiwork.

P. Lynn Denton
Texas Memorial Museum

BRODERIE

Les broderies du Maroc témoignent éloquemment du désir humain de jouir des articles de beauté dans la vie quotidienne. Créée principalement dans les villes de Rabat, Salé, Meknès, Fès, Tétouan, Chichaoua, et Azemmour, la broderie au Maroc est un phénomème urbain qui reflète le flux et le reflux des peuples islamiques et non-islamiques et les influences de l'Andalusie, la Méditerranée, et d'autres régions de l'Afrique du Nord. Les réfugiés de la reconquête chrétienne de l'Espagne, la conquête portugaise de certaines parties du littoral marocain, la pression de l'expansion turque à partir de l'est, et l'occupation française ont chacun influencé le caractère et l'art de la broderie au Maroc durant les derniers 4 à 5 siècles. Beaucoup des influences externes sur les motifs et techniques transmises pendant cette histoire ont des antécédents dans les périodes Classique et Byzantine. Cependant, les exemples qui survivent ne répresentent que le 18ème au 20ème siècles. Dans les mêmes régions, la population berbère indigène maintenait une tradition de tissage séparée et distincte.

Les femmes des communautés arabes et juives ornaient les textiles de ménage et les vêtements avec de la broderie de fils de soie et métalliques. On utilisait des motifs de broderie pour décorer des mobiliers tels que les taies d'oreillers et couvertures de matelas, rideaux, tentures aux murs et aux portes, châles, écharpes, voiles pour les bains, napperons et mouchoirs. Les motifs sur ces articles étaient brodés avec de la bourre de soie détordue sur une toile de fond de cotton ou de lin. Les écharpes ou mouchoirs très fins avaient un tissu de fond de soie. Des couleurs et choix de points de broderies particuliers caractérisaient chaque ville. Par exemple, les broderies de Chichaoua sont multicolores avec des répétitions géométriques organisées en paneaux de motifs, tandis que les anciennes broderies de Rabat consistent souvent en un dense motif floral bleu, rouge ou violet monochrome. Les motifs de broderie de Fès comprennent une technique à jour de fils comptés reversibles, qui incorpore le tissu de fond comme grille pour le travail d'aiguille complété. Les broderies d'Azemmour reflètent les motifs de la Renaissance italienne et espagnole dans le sens que le motif est créé par l'image négative qui reste après qu'on ait recouvert le fond de points comptés (comme dans le travail d'Asissi). Les choix de motifs comptent des chimères, griffons, oiseaux autour d'un vase central, et des femmes stylisées avec les bras en l'air et des longues jupes triangulaires. A Rabat et Tétouan, on dessine souvent les motifs à main levée et ensuite on les couvre de points. Le plumetis, le point de tige, le point de chausson, le point de reprise, et le point de croix de marquage à face double sont les plus courants. Un cadre de broderie de type turc était utilisé dans certains endroits, comme à Fès, tandis que dans d'autres régions on utilisait la méthode espagnole d'épingler le tissu à un coussin bien bourré qu'on tenait sur les genoux.

Les brodeuses juives de Tétouan produisaient des broderies de fils d'or particulièrement fines et élaborées pour les habits. Le costume de mariage, qui comprenait un gilet boléro, une large ceinture et une jupe portefeuille, était décoré de boutons très ornés et de broderie d'or, et faisait partie de la dot de la mariée. Fès est aussi un centre renommé de broderie d'or. La broderie de fils d'or et d'argent est d'habitude exécutée sur du velours ou du cuir, et orne le plus souvent des ceintures, coussins, couvertures du Coran, chaussures et chapeaux. D'autres articles brodés d'or sont les "haitis" ou tentures de murs utilisées dans les maisons et les tentes, et conçues comme des séries de motifs d'arches reliées, soit brodées en or sur velours, soit fabriquées par une technique d'application. (illus.p. 100)

Ce sont les femmes qui font la broderie. Les hommes finissent la fabrication des bourses, pantoufles et chapeaux. La broderie des selles, pour laquelle Fès est très connue, est particulièrement difficile et elle est entreprise par les hommes, tandis que les tapis et sacoches de selle sont décorés par les femmes. Les hommes et les femmes fabriquent les galons, glands et garnitures. De tels embellissements peuvent être ajoutés comme garnitures aux tissus de brocart très ornés, tissés de soie et de fils métalliques pour fabriquer des ceintures, des caftans de femmes et des tapisseries (illus. p. 100, 101). Les hommes dans ces ateliers tissent des motifs complexes sur des métiers jacquards à partir de dessins marocains traditionnels ou dérivés des cultures islamiques-andalouses et des influences européenes. Les ceintures de ce type combinent quatre motifs ou plus, d'habitude avec des bandes géométriques et florales alternantes. On les porte pliées en deux dans le sens de la longueur et enroulées autour de la taille, et on peut changer de ceinture simplement en l'enroulant de façon différente ou en la retournant de l'autre côté. Des tissus de fond de ce genre pourraient être encore embellis de broderie.

On apprenait aux jeunes femmes à broder comme apprenties à une brodeuse experte, ou ma'allema. Cet individu fournissait de l'instruction en échange de paiements ou de cadeaux, et pourrait être une parente ou amie. Comme dans d'autres parties du monde, les étudiantes produisaient des marques pour démontrer leur maîtrise des techniques et pour rappeler des motifs et points. Pourtant, contrairement à leurs contreparties européennes et américaines, les marocaines incluaient rarement des exemples calligraphiques. On passait parfois une commande aux ma'allema habilles de créer des motifs à forme libre ou d'exécuter un article particulier, bien que la plupart des Marocaines fassent de la broderie pour leur usage personnel.

Comme dans les autres arts à base domestique, la créativité, les préférences personnelles et l'excellence technique étaient toutes exprimées par la brodeuse marocaine individuelle. Par contraste à la simple facade extérieure du foyer séparant la famille du monde extérieur, le travail de l'aiguille d'une femme fournissait un monde intérieur coloré et vibrant, et définissait sa signification et ses traditions par son ouvrage.

RESUME

The collection used in Resplendent Diversity originated from the Texas Memorial Museum in Austin, Texas, with Dr.William Reeder as the Director and Lynn Denton as the Curator.

Lynn Denton est Directrice adjoint et Conservatrice d'Anthropologie et d'Histoire à Texas Memorial Museum, un musée d'histoire naturale et culturale établi en commémoration du centenaire de Texas en 1936, et situé au campus de l'Université de Texas à Austin. Ses intérêts professionals incluent, principalement, la recherche sur les textiles ethnographiques et l'histoire textile, y inclut les techniques, les matériaux, et leur contexte cultural. Elle se spécialise dans ce domaine pour son doctorat en anthropologie culturale à UT. La collection utilisée dans Diversité resplendissante, est venue du Texas Memorial Museum, à Austin Texas, avec Dr.William Reeder, Directeur, et Lynn Denton, Conservatrice.

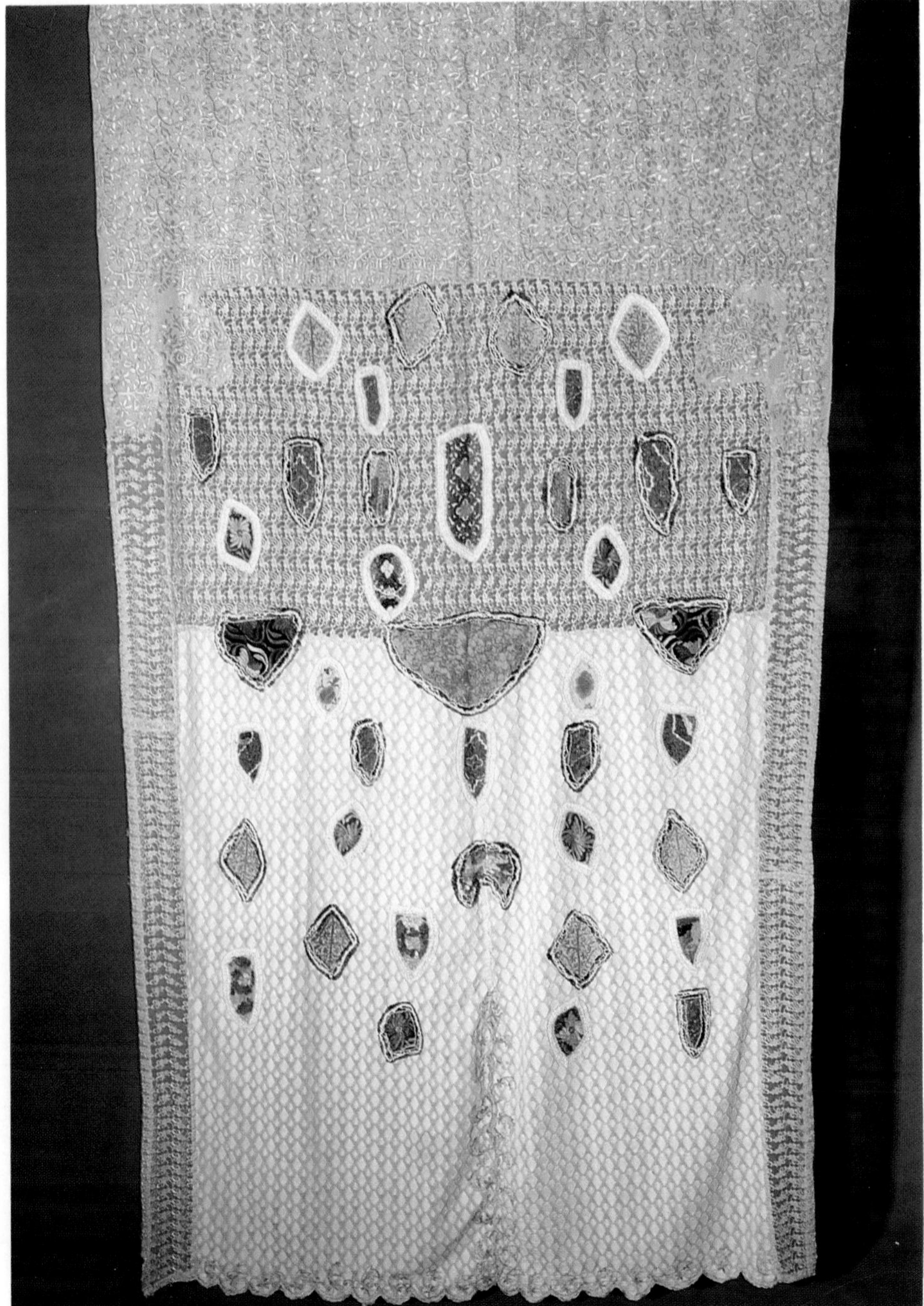

Photo: Grant

Embroidery: Silk on silk, 5' x 12', Early 20th Century, previously displayed in a synagogue. AMMA.
Broderie: soie sur soie, début du 20ème siècle, exposée précédemment dans une synagogue. AMMA.

Photo: Author

The American Museum of Moroccan Art (AMMA). Tucson, Arizona, USA.
Le Musée américain d'Art marocain (AMMA). Tucson, Arizona, Etats-Unis.

American Museum of Moroccan Art

The American Museum of Moroccan Art is a small museum and Moroccan rug shop located in Tucson, Arizona. Although the museum hosts a constantly changing exhibit of Moroccan textiles and artifacts, its primary functions are more varied.

The museum is a routing office for more extensive Moroccan museum exhibitions, such as the previously shown "Resplendent Diversity" exhibition. The AMMA conducts tours to Morocco and acts as an information center for Americans visiting Morocco and Moroccan tourists visiting the United States.

For information concerning museum activities, contact the AMMA at Box 50472, Tucson, Arizona, 85703-1472, USA. Tel: 602-529-0232 FAX: 602-529-2791

Moroccan National Tourist Offices:
20 E. 46th St., # 1201, New York, NY 10017
421 N. Rodeo Dr., Beverly Hills, CA 90210
Morocco Epcot Center
Lake Buena Vista, FL 32830

In Canada:
20001 rue Université, Suite 1460
Montréal, PQH 3A 2A6

Musée américain d'Art marocain

Le Musée américain d'Art marocain est un petit musée et magasin de tapis marocains à Tucson, Arizona. Bien que le musée expose des exhibitions de textiles et d'objets fabriqués du Maroc qui changent constamment, ses fonctions primaires sont plus variées.

Ce musée est un bureau d'organisation pour des exhibitions marocaines plus étendues, telle que l'exhibition récente de "Diversité resplendissante." L'AMMA conduit des tours du Maroc et fonctionne comme un centre d'informations pour les Américains visitant le Maroc et les Marocains visitant les Etats-Unis.

Pour plus d'informations au sujet des activités du musée, veuillez vous adresser à: AMMA at Box 50472, Tucson, Arizona 85703-1472, USA. Tel: 602-529-0232 FAX: 602-529-2791

Offices Nationaux Marocains de Tourisme:
Au Canada:
20001 rue Université, Suite 1460,
Montréal, PQH 3A 2A6

A Paris, l'Ambassade du Maroc se trouve à:
5 rue la Tasse, 75106, Paris, France.
Paris a aussi un Office National Marocain de Tourisme.

Photo: Author

AMMA associate Steve Moore examines a table top in the museum.
Steve Moore, associé de l'AMMA, examine un dessus de table dans le musée.

Photo: Author

AMMA tour coordinators Jerry Whitney and David Moore prepare information packets.
Jerry Whitney et David Moore, coordinateurs des tours de l'AMMA, preparent des paquets d'informations.

Photo: Author

Max Drachman of Tucson, Arizona, checks out the children's room at the AMMA.
Max Drachman de Tucson, Arizona, visite la salle d'enfants à l'AMMA.

Photo: Author

Learning through fun: The Children's Room. AMMA.
Apprendre en s'amusant: la salle d'enfants. AMMA.

Photo: Author

AMMA Conservation Staff members Rick Busselle and Chris Taylor: The never-ending chore.
Rick Busselle et Chris Taylor, membres du personnel de conservation de l'AMMA: la tâche sans fin.

Ancient Islamic illumination: Cursive script. *Ancienne enluminure islamique: écriture cursive.*

Illuminations–The Ancient Islamic Art of Ornamenting and Gilding Manuscripts

Pages of the Koran, historical documents, astronomy, alchemy, mathematics, music and others were previously conserved. These specimens, the oldest dating back to the 12th century, are conserved in the Royal Al Hassania Library in Rabat.

L'enluminure: l'ancien art de la l'ornement et de la dorure des manuscrits.

Pages de Coran, documents d'histoire, d'astronomie, d'alchimie, de mathématiques, de musique, et autres ont été conservés. Ces specimens, dont le plus ancien date du 12ème siècle, sont conservés dans la bibliothèque royale Al Hassania de Rabat.

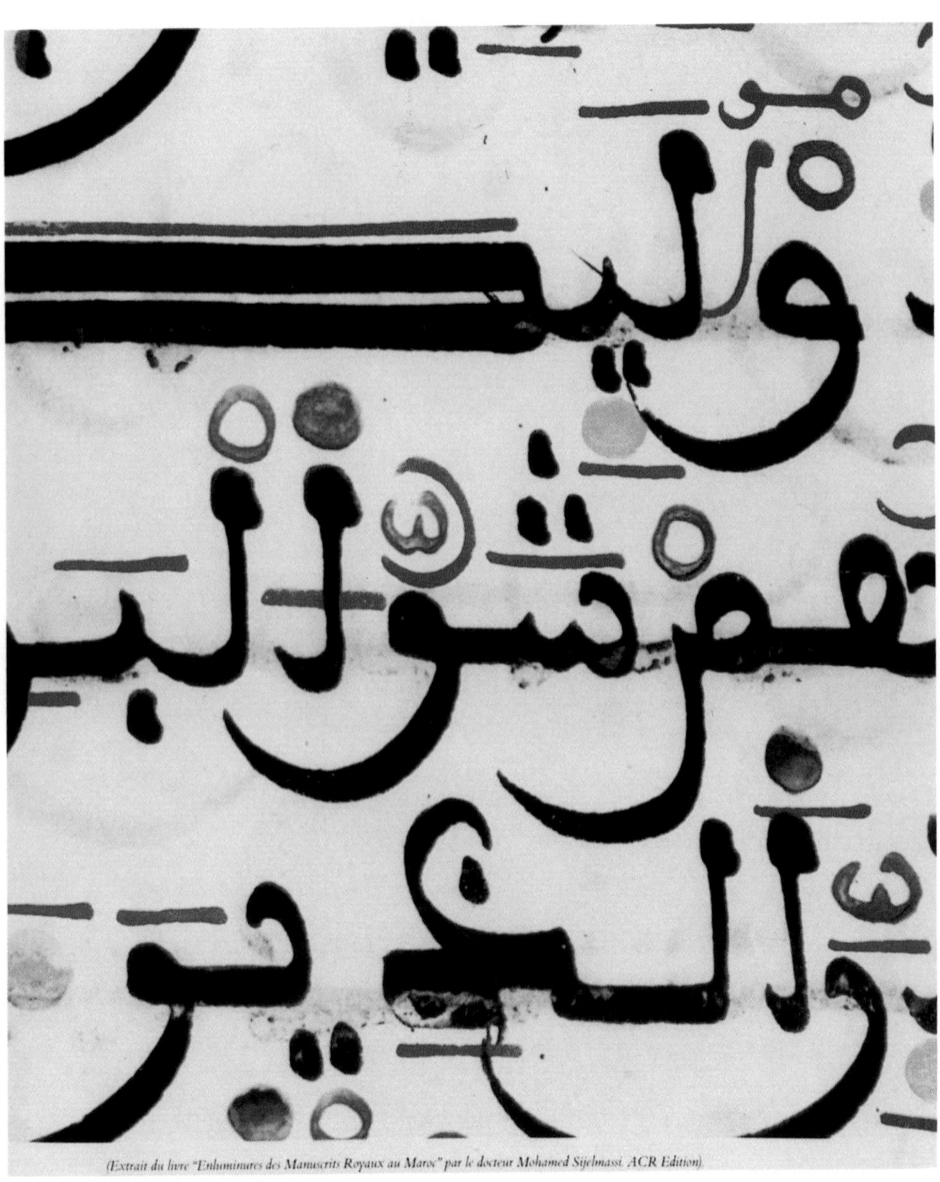

(Extrait du livre "Enluminures des Manuscrits Royaux au Maroc" par le docteur Mohamed Sijelmassi. ACR Edition).

Ancient Islamic illumination: Kufic calligraphy.
Ancienne enluminure islamique: calligraphie koufie.

Ancient Islamic illumination: Maghribi script.
Ancienne enluminure islamique: script maghribi.

Massive marble pillar with hand-carved plaster designs. Photo: Author
Massive colonne de marbre avec motifs en stuc ouvragés à la main.

Designed by the King, A Wonder of the Modern World Takes Form in Casablanca The Grand Mosque of Hassan II

In Casablanca, Morocco's largest and most cosmopolitan city, 4-1/2 million people are witnessing the construction of the third largest mosque in the world. Only Mecca and Medina, the centers of Islam, have larger ones.

2,500 on-site workers, under the direction of French architect Michel Pinseau, are working with more than 8,000 artisans in shops throughout Morocco, and thousands of tons of pink and green Moroccan marble, sculptured and polished, now sit atop gigantic granite pillars from Southern Morocco.

The first step was to push back the sea and build a dike, to let the ground harden. After completion, the dike will be removed to allow the ocean to flow under two-thirds of the prayer hall. A raised walkway will allow entrance into the grand hall from all sides.

The ceiling in the grand hall is 40 meters high. A touch of a button opens it to the sky above. Inside, 20,000 people can pray at one time, with room for another 80,000 on the esplanade.

The minaret is 625 square meters wide at its base and 200 meters high. It's the only minaret in the world that gives access to the underneath areas of the tower. Laser beams, shining from the top of the minaret, will be seen from as far as 30 miles away. Other buildings in the complex, once completed, will include a museum and a library. There is parking underneath for 1,100 cars. Roadways are connected by 800 meters of underground tunnels.

Throughout Morocco, people feel an immense sense of pride about the Mosque. The country's finest sculptors, tile workers, mosaic artists, metal workers, and wood carvers will add the finishing touches to Morocco's greatest treasure—the Grand Mosque of Hassan II.

Photo: Author

The Grand Mosque of Hassan II, Casablanca, Morocco. *La grande mosquée de Hassan II, Casablanca, Maroc.*

Conçu par le roi, une merveille du monde moderne prend forme à Casablanca La grande mosquée de Hassan II

A Casablanca, la ville la plus grande et la plus cosmopolite du Maroc, 4,5 millions d'hommes, femmes et enfants sont témoins à la construction de la troisième mosquée la plus grande du monde, suivant seulement celles de la Mecque et Médine, les centres de l'Islam.

2.500 ouvriers sur le site travaillent avec 8.000 artisans dans des ateliers à travers le Maroc, sous la direction de l'architecte français Michel Pinseau, et des milliers de tonnes de marbre marocain rose et vert sculpté et poli reposent maintenant sur des gigantiques colonnes de granite du Maroc méridional.

Le premier pas de la construction fut de repousser la mer et de construire une digue pour permettre à la terre de durcir. Une fois que la mosquée est construite, on enlèvera la digue pour permettre à l'océan de circuler sous les deux tiers de la salle des prières. Un passage pour piétons élevé donnera accès à la grande salle de tous les côtés.

Le plafond de la grande salle est à 40 mètres de haut. Il s'ouvre au ciel quand on touche un bouton. A l'intérieur, 20.000 personnes peuvent prier en même temps, et il y a de la place pour 80.000 de plus sur l'esplanade.

Le minaret mesure 625 mètres carrés à sa base et culmine à 200 mètres de haut. C'est le seul minaret au monde où l'on peut accéder à l'espace sous la tour. Un phare à lasers, brillant du sommet du minaret, sera visible à jusqu'à 35 kilomètres.

Une fois complété, le complexe contiendra aussi un musée et une bibliothèque. Il y aura un parking en-dessous pour 1.100 voitures, et 800 mètres de tunnels souterrains le relieront aux chaussées.

Le gens sont très fiers de cette mosquée partout dans le Maroc. Les meilleurs sculpteurs, artisans de zelliges et de mosaïques, ferroniers et sculpteurs de bois du pays mettront la dernière main au plus grand trésor du Maroc: la grande mosquée de Hassan II.

Hand-carved mandalic designs decorate the ceilings.
Photo: Author
Des dessins en forme de mandalas sculptés à la main ornent les plafonds.

Photo: Author

The ceiling opening and sea wall as seen from the minaret.
L'ouverture du plafond et la digue comme vues du minaret.

Photo: Author

Granite pillars from Southern Morocco will break the waves.
Des pilliers de granite du Maroc du Sud vont couper les vagues.

Photo: Author

A model with open ceiling shows the complex with the library, university and museum.
Un modèle à plafond ouvert montre l'ensemble avec la bibliothèque, l'université et le musée.

Photo: Author

A hand-inlaid mosaic tile mirhab made of natural stones.
Mirhab de mosaïques de pierres naturelles incrustées à la main.

Photo: Author

Islamic architecture at its finest, in pink Moroccan marble.
Le sommet de l'architecture islamique en marbre rose marocain.

Photo: Author

A worker's car lends perspective to the size of the structure.
La voiture d'un ouvrier met en perspective la taille de la structure.

Photo: Author

Above: A labyrinth of scaffolding built to accommodate the 2,500 on-site workers.
Un labyrinthe d'échafaudage construit pour les 2.500 ouvriers sur le site.

Opposite: A hallway of gigantic hand-carved arches. Photo: Author
Un couloir d'arches gigantesques sculptées à la main.

Photo: Author

Wood, plaster and metal sculptured harmoniously create the balconies.
Le bois, le plâtre et le métal sculptés harmonieusement créent des balcons.

Photo: J. Taylor

Above: Separate men's and women's bathing areas. Each accommodate up to 700 people.
Coins séparés pour les bains des hommes et des femmes. Chacun peut contenir jusqu' à 700 personnes.

Opposite: Hand-carved pillars of cedar are used for support and decoration. Photo: Author
Des colonnes de bois de cèdre sculptées à la main pour le soutien et la décoration.

Photo: Author

Mosaic patterns of ...
Mosaïques de...

Photo: Author

Photo: Author

...wood, tile and paint
...bois, zelliges, et peinture

Photo: Author

Photo: Author

Photo: Author

Opposite: Koranic scriptures adorn a hand-founded brass door. Photo: Author
Des Ecritures saintes du Coran ornent une porte en laiton fondue à la main.

إنما يعمر مسجد الله من آمن بالله واليوم الآخر
بسم الله الرحمن الرحيم

Photo: J. Taylor

Alf Taylor and Ambassador Michael Ussery in the Grand Mosque.
Alf Taylor et l'ambassadeur Michael Ussery dans la grande mosquée.

My thanks to His Excellency Ambassador Michael Ussery for the idea of including the Grand Mosque of Hassan II in this book. Ambassador Ussery also obtained the permission needed, and took time away from his busy schedule to escort me through this magnificent structure. My personal thanks to Michael for extending his South Carolina-bred hospitality to Judi and me at his home in Rabat. My thanks to his wife, Betsy, for her graciousness at Villa America, for sharing Gregory with us, and for her efforts in making a difference in Morocco. To Falih, Latifa, Fattah, Halima, Kabira and the others who made Villa America so comfortable for Judi and me: you will always be welcome in our home.

I'd also like to thank Mr. Horache Kaddour for guiding Ambassador Ussery, myself and our party through the Grand Mosque. The information provided by Mr. Horache made this chapter possible.

Je voudrais remercier Son Excellence Monsieur l'Ambassadeur Michael Ussery de son idée d'inclure la grande mosquée de Hassan II dans ce livre. Monsieur Ussery a aussi obtenu la permission nécessaire et a consacré beaucoup de son temps précieux à m'accompagner durant ma visite à cette magnifique structure. Je voudrais exprimer mes remerciements personnels à Michael d'avoir offert à Judi et moi son hospitalité typique de la Caroline du Sud à sa maison à Rabat. Je voudrais aussi remercier sa femme Betsy de sa bienveillance à la Villa America, de nous avoir fait connaître Gregory, et de ses efforts pour améliorer les choses au Maroc. A Salih, Latifa, Fattah, Halima, Kabira et aux autres qui ont rendu la Villa America si comfortable pour Judi et moi: vous serez toujours les bienvenus chez nous.

Je voudrais aussi remercier M. Horache Kaddour d'avoir guidé l'ambassadeur, notre groupe et moi à travers la grande mosquée. Les informations fournies par M. Horache m'ont permis d'écrire ce chapitre.

The Royal Palace, Rabat. *Photo: Author*
Le palais royal, Rabat.

Museums and Monuments in the Imperial Cities - Rabat, Meknes, Fez, Marrakech

Musées et monuments des villes impériales - Rabat, Meknès, Fès, Marrakech

Mausoleum of Mohammed V, Rabat.
Mausolée de Mohammed V, Rabat.
Photo: Hahn

Rabat

The Capital City of Rabat is situated on the Atlantic Ocean at the mouth of the Bu Regreg River, across from the City of Salé. A good view of the two cities can be obtained from Hassan Tower. The "petit taxi" drivers in Rabat are quite aware of what the tourists want to see, and the Moroccan tourist offices are helpful. They are in the vicinity of Place Abraham Lincoln and Rue P. Lumumba.

The Hassan Tower and the Masoleum of Mohammed V

The minaret known as Hassan Tower in 53 feet wide, 144 feet high and has walls 8 feet thick. It sits on a complex 40 meters wide and 135 meters long, on the site of the Mosque of Hassan. Its construction was begun in 1197 by the Third Caliph Almohade Abou Yousseff Yacoub Al Mansour, but it was never completed.

Rabat

Rabat, la capitale, est située sur l'océan Atlantique à l'embouchure du fleuve Bouregreg, en face de la ville de Salé. On peut obtenir une bonne vue des deux villes à partir de la tour Hassan. Les chauffeurs de "petits taxis" à Rabat sont très au courant de ce que les touristes désirent voir, et les Offices de Tourisme Marocains sont très obligeants. Ils se trouvent dans les environs de la place Abraham Lincoln et la rue P. Lumumba.

La tour Hassan et le mausolée de Mohammed V

Le minaret qu'on appelle la tour Hassan est large de 16 mètres et haut de 43 mètres; ses murs ont une épaisseur de 2,5 mètres. Il se trouve dans un complexe large de 40 mètres et long de 135 mètres, sur le site de la mosquée d'Hassan. Sa construction fut entamée en 1197 par le troisième Caliphe Almohade Abou Youssef Yacoub Al Mansour, mais ne fut jamais achevée.

Photo: Hahn

Photo: Hahn

Hand-carved ceiling/a holy man says prayers beside the onyx sarcophagus-Tomb of Mohammed V, Rabat.
Plafond sculpté à la main/un saint homme dit des prières à côté du sarcophage d'onyx. Tombeau de Mohammed V, Rabat.

Beyond the 200 broken columns of the ancient mosque, the Mausoleum and Mosque of Mohammed V rise from the terrace. This inspiring example of Islamic architecture was designed by the architect Vo Toan. (see p. 130)

The Royal Palace, Avenue Yacoub Al Mansour. Check for tour times.

Chellah Gardens, referred to as the most romantic place in Morocco. The Chellah is the ultimate picture of Moroccan serenity.

Kasbah and Museum of the Oudaias: The Kasbah (old city) of the Oudaia gives you a view of Rabat and Salé as they were at the beginning of their history. It is also a great place to stroll on your way to the Museum Gardens of the Oudaias, and it has a charming café overlooking the river. Remember to go quietly... you are visiting someone's neighborhood!

The Archeological Museum: in the Vicinity of Avenue Moulay Hassan and Avenue Allal Ben Abdullah. The museum features objects from the main archaeological settlements in the country, and a large royal white marble jewel-encrusted statue.

The Ensemble Artisanal (see p. 20).

The Museum of Moroccan Arts, located across the street from the Ensemble Artisanal.

The Museum of Traditional Crafts, just east of the Museum of Moroccan Arts.

The Great Mosque of Rabat, in the vicinity of the Avenues Yacoub Al Mansour and Moulay Hassan.

The Great Mosque of Salé, located in the Medina of Salé.

The Scientific Institute and the Forests and Water Institutes.

Medersa (Koranic School) El Hassan, located in Salé.

Some of the better known beaches in the vicinity of Rabat are Little Smugglers, Temara, Golden Valley, Krick Rock, Golden Sands, Skhirat and Oued Ykem. As is the rule on beaches everywhere, investigate the swimming conditions carefully.

Au-delà des 200 colonnes tronquées de l'ancienne mosquée, le mausolée et la mosquée de Mohammed V s'élèvent de la terrace. Cet exemple inspirant d'architecture islamique fut conçu par l'architecte Vo Toan.

Le Palais Royal, avenue Yacoub Al Mansour. Verifiez l'horaire des tours.

Les Jardins de Chellah, qu'on appelle le coin le plus romantique du Maroc. Ces jardins sont l'ultime image de la sérénité marocaine.

La Kasbah et le Musée des Oudaias: la Kasbah (vieille ville) de l'Oudaia vous donnera un bon aperçu de Rabat et Salé tels qu'ils étaient au début de leur histoire. C'est aussi un endroit magnifique pour se promener en allant au Musée et aux Jardins des Oudaias, et il y a là un charmant café donnant sur le fleuve. Souvenez-vous de ne pas faire trop de bruit: c'est un quartier résidentiel!

Le Musée archéologique: près de l'angle de l'avenue Moulay Hassan et l'avenue Allal Ben Abdullah. Le musée exhibe des objects provenant des principaux sites archéologiques du pays, et expose une grande statue royale de marbre blanc incrustée de bijoux.

L'ensemble Artisanal (voir p. 20).

Le Musée des Arts marocains, situé en face de l'Ensemble Artisanal.

Le Musée d'Artisanat traditionnel, juste à l'ouest du Musée d'Arts marocains.

La grande mosquée de Rabat, près de l'angle de l'avenue Yakoub Al Mansour et l'avenue Moulay Hassan.

La grande mosquée de Salé, située dans la médine de Salé.

L'Institut Scientifique et l'Institut des Eaux et Forêts.

Medersa (université coranique) El Hassan, à Salé.

Voici quelques-unes des plages assez connues aux environs de Rabat: Petits Contrebandiers, Temara, Vallée d'Or, Krick Rock, Sables dorés, Skhirat et Oued Ykem. Comme pour toutes les plages, il faut se renseigner soigneusement sur les conditions de natation.

Photo: Sisk

"The Waterman," oil, by Duane Bryers. Sonoita, Arizona, USA.
"Le vendeur d'eau," huile, par Duane Bryers. Sonoita, Arizona, Etats-Unis.

Fez

Fez, the oldest of Morocco's imperial cities, is divided into two sections. The old city, Fez El Bali, founded by Idriss II in 809 and the new city, Fez El Jedid, are situated in the foothills of the Middle Atlas Mountains. Fez has the look of an ancient Islamic city. It has always been the intellectual, cultural and religious center of Morocco.

The Fez Tourist Office is located at the Place de Résistance. The City Information Bureau is located at the Place Mohammed V.

Fez Cultural Sights:
Dar El Batha Museum - Moroccan Arts Museum, located at the Place de l'Istiqlal
Gardens of Boujeloud
Dar El Beïda Palace
Medersa Bou Anania
The El Qarawiyin Mosque - built in 859
The Andalusian Mosque - built in 861
The Zaouiya of Moulay Idriss
The Facade of the Royal Palace
Jnane Sbile Garden
Nejjarin Fountain
Medersa Attarine
Medersa Al Seffarin
Medersa Al Cherratin
The Marinid Tombs
The Hamra Mosque
The Royal Palace, located in the vicinity of the Place des Alaouites
Some interesting gates to see are the Bab Slender (gate of the Saddlers), Bab Al Khemis, on the road to Rabat, and Bab Mansour.
Side-trips from Fez:
The Moulay Yacoub and Sidi Harazen Thermal Hot Springs Resorts
The Arms Museum, located in the Medieval fortress Borj Nord
Kasbah des Cherarda, dating from the 17th Century and located in the vicinity of Tour des Fes Nord
The Bin-el-Ouidane Dam
The Ouzoud Waterfalls
The charming towns of Ifrane, Azrou and Kenitra

Fès

Fès, la plus ancienne des villes impériales du Maroc, est divisé en deux sections. La vieille ville, Fès El Bali, fut fondée par Idriss II en 809, et la nouvelle ville, Fès El Jedid, sont situées dans les contreforts du Moyen Atlas. Fès a l'apparence d'une ancienne ville islamique, et a toujours été le centre intellectuel, culturel et religieux du Maroc.

L'Office de Tourisme de Fès est situé sur la place de la Résistance. L'Office d'Informations de la Ville est situé sur la place Mohammed V.

Attractions culturelles de Fès:
Musée Dar El Batha - musée d'arts marocains, sur la place de l'Istiqlal
Jardins de Boujeloud
Palais Dar El Beïda
Medersa Bou Anania

"Fez Medina," watercolor, by Nancy Boren. Dallas, Texas, USA.
"Médina de Fès," aquarelle, par Nancy Boren. Dallas, Texas, Etats-Unis.

Mosquée El Qarawiyin - bâtie en 859
Mosquée andalouse- bâtie en 861
Zaouiya de Moulay Idriss
Facade du Palais Royal
Jardin Jnane Sbile
Fontaine Nejjarin
Medersa Attarine
Medersa Al Seffarin
Medersa Al Cherratin
Tombeaux des Mérinides
Mosquée Hamra
Le Palais Royal, situé aux environs de la place des Alaouites

Il y a quelques portes intéressantes à Fès, y compris les portes Bab Slender (portes des selliers), Bab Al Khemis sur la route de Rabat, et Bab Mansour.

Petites excursions à partir de Fès:
Les stations balnéaires des sources thermales de Moulay Yacoub et Sidi Harazen
Le Musée des Armes, dans la forteresse médiévale de Borj Nord
La Kasbah des Cherarda, datant du 17ème siècle et située près de la Tour de Fès Nord
Le Barrage Bin-el-Ouidane
Les Cascades d'Ouzoud
Les villes charmantes d'Ifrane, Azrou et Kenitra

Photo: Hahn

Fez Medina (old city), the largest in Africa.
Médina de Fès (vieille ville), la plus grande de l'Afrique.

Photo: Hahn

Bou Inania Medersa, 1350-1357 AD, the oldest active university in Africa. Fez.
Medersa Bou Inania, 1350-1357 de notre ère, la plus ancienne université active de l'Afrique. Fès.

Shrine of Mulai Idriss II, Founder of Fez.
Lieu saint de Mulai Idriss II, fondateur de Fès.

Meknes

The name "Meknes" is derived from the Meknassa, the Berber tribe who founded Taza and Meknes. In 1673, it was selected as the capital by the great Alaouit Sultan Moulay Ismail. The colossal Bab Mansour Gate is one of the outstanding monuments here. It was finished around 1732 and is one of the most famous gates in all of North Africa.

The tourist information office will have more specific information on the sights in Meknes. It is located in the vicinity of the Esplanade de la Foire.

Meknes Cultural Sights
The Ben Aissa Tomb
The Berdaine Mosque, near the Place el Berdaine
The Royal Palace
Dar Jamai, near the Place al-Hedim
The Great Mosque
The Granaries
Medersa Bou Inania
Medersa Filada
The Stables of Sultan Moulay Ismail
The Masoleum of Moulay Ismail

Some interesting places to visit around Meknes are the Holy City of Moulay Idriss and the Roman ruins of Volubilis. The spa city of Oulmes is also a nice place for a one-day outing.

Meknès

Le nom "Meknès" est dérivé des Meknassa, une tribu berbère qui avait fondé Taza et Meknès. En 1673, cette ville fut choisie comme la capitale par le grand sultan alaouite Moulay Ismail. Les portes colossales Bab Mansour sont un des monuments exceptionnels ici. Complétées vers 1732, et elles se classent parmi les portes les plus connues de toute l'Afrique du Nord.

L'Office National Marocain du Tourisme vous fournira des renseignements plus spécifiques sur les attractions de Meknès. Cet office est situé près de l'Esplanade de la Foire.

Attractions culturelles de Meknès
Le tombeau de Ben Aissa
La mosquée Berdaine, près de la place el Berdaine
Le palais royal
Dar Jamai, près de la place al-Hedim
La grande mosquée
Les greniers à blé
Medersa Bou Inania
Medersa Filada
Les écuries du Sultan Moulay Ismail
Le mausolée de Moulay Ismail

D'autres endroits intéressants à visiter autour de Meknès sont la Ville Sainte de Moulay Idriss et les ruines romaines de Volubilis. La ville d'eau d'Oulmès est également une bonne destination pour une excursion d'une journée.

Photo: Sisk

"Meknes," French railroad poster, Bab Mansour Gate. Brondy, 1927.
"Meknès," affiche de chemin de fer française, portes de Bab Mansour. Brondy, 1927.

Photo: Bertrand-Marrakesh

Gate: Bab El Berdaine, XVIII Century, Meknes.
Portes: Bab El Berdaine, XVIII siècle, Meknès.

Photo: Hahn

Stables of Sultan Moulay Ismail, 1673 AD, 12,000 horses, Meknes.
Ecuries du Sultan Moulay Ismail, 1673 de notre ère, 12.000 chevaux, Meknès.

Photo: Hahn

Underground stables of Moulay Ismail, Meknes.
Ecuries souterraines de Moulay Ismail, Meknès.

"Marrakesh Marketplace," watercolor, by Tom Hill, Tucson, Arizona, USA.
"Marché de Marrakech," aquarelle, par Tom Hill, Tucson, Arizona, Etats-Unis.

Marrakesh

Marrakesh has had many unofficial but well-deserved titles throughout the years, such as "Pearl of the South" and "City of Earthly Delights."

Marrakesh was founded in the 11th Century by the Almoravid Berber chieftain Abou Bekr. Enriched with booty from a Spanish raid, Marrakesh was the trading center of Morocco through the latter part of the 11th century.

Marrakesh is the Great City of the Berbers. It has successfully preserved the pure medieval structure that existed during the period when it was founded.

Marrakech

Marrakech a jouit de plusieurs noms non officiels mais bien mérités au cours des années, tels que "la Perle du Sud" et "la Ville des délices terrestres."

Marrakech fut fondé à l'onzième siècle par le chef des Berbères Almoravides, Abou Bekr. Enrichi de butin provenant d'un raid dans l'Espagne, Marrakech fut le centre commercial du Maroc durant les dernières années du onzième siècle.

Marrakech est la Grande Ville des Berbères, et a réussi à préserver la structure médiévale pure qui y existait au moment de sa fondation.

Photo: Author

Cobra charmer Hadj Bouchaib: place Jemaa-el-Fna, Marrakesh.
Hadj Bouchaib, charmeur de cobras: place Jemaa-el-Fna, Marrakech.

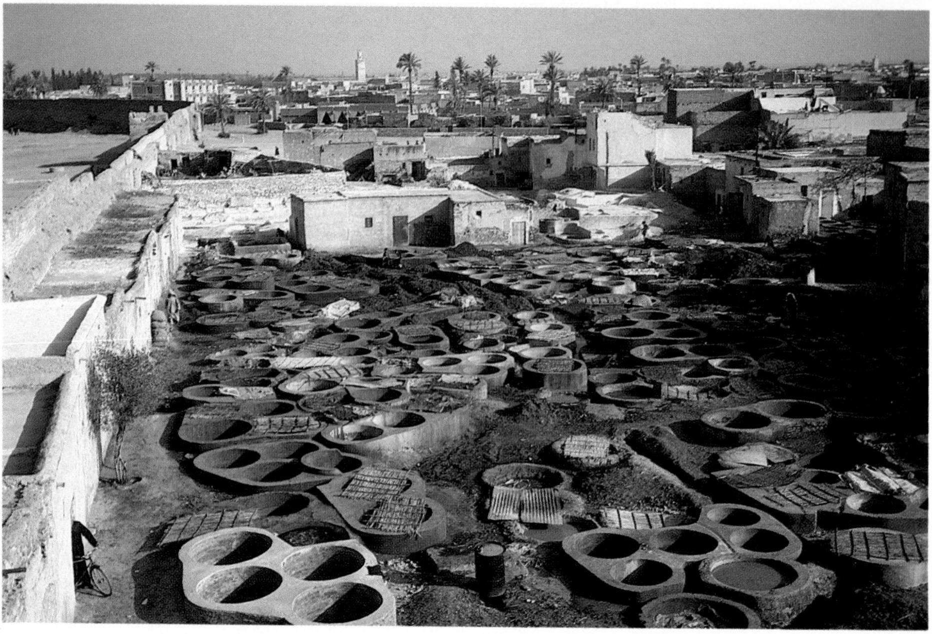

Photo: Hahn

Leather tannery: Take some mint for your nose. Marrakesh.
Tannerie de cuir: prenez de la menthe pour votre nez. Marrakech.

Photo: Hahn

The souks of Marrakesh.
Les souks de Marrakech.

Marrakesh

Marrakesh has had many unofficial but well-deserved titles throughout the years, such as "Pearl of the South" and "City of Earthly Delights."

Marrakesh was founded in the 11th Century by the Almoravid Berber chieftain Abou Bekr. Enriched with booty from a Spanish raid, Marrakesh was the trading center of Morocco through the latter part of the 11th century.

Marrakesh is the Great City of the Berbers. It has successfully preserved the pure medieval structure that existed during the period when it was founded.

Today Marrakesh is a thriving, highly energetic cultural city where tourism prevails. It is divided into two sections: The old city, or Medina, where throngs of pedestrians jam the small streets winding through the marketplaces, just as they have for centuries; and the new section, called Gueliz, where the French have left their mark. The streets in Gueliz are wide, and modern sidewalk cafés serve cuisine from all over the world. Banks, tourist offices, bookstores, airline agencies: In Gueliz you'll find all the comforts of the 20th century.

The two cities, which are about a mile apart, are linked together by the Avenue Mohammed V. It is on this street, in the center of Gueliz, that you'll find the local tourist office.

The Koutoubia Minaret (Remember, non-Moslems and prying cameras are not permitted.) There's no better place to start than with this most revered Moroccan Mosque. The name "Koutoubia" comes from the Arabic word Kutubbiyyin, meaning "book" or "library." The mosque has always had a library connected to it and at one time it housed a copy of the Koran which the Marinid Sultan Abu Al-Mumim had brought back from Cordoba. It had belonged to Uthman Ibn Affan, the third orthodox caliph, and contained four prayers in his own script. This book was lost at sea in the 13th century. (see p. 192)

The Place Jemaa-el-Fna (assembly of the dead) is Marrakesh's most famous tourist attraction, and for a good reason. The Jemaa-el-Fna is a huge open area at the main entrance of the Medina. Gathered here are story-tellers, dancers, acrobats, snake charmers, fire-eaters, soothsayers, medicine men and animal acts, all performing for coins, as they have for centuries. Keep a close eye on your pocketbook, but enjoy the show.

The Saadian tombs were built by Ahmed Al Mansour in 1578 as a burial place for the Saadian Royal Family. They were walled up around 1700 by Moulay Ismail and rediscovered two hundred years later, in 1911. Sixty-two Sultans, their wives and children were buried here, with more than a hundred other graves in the courtyard.

The Bahia Palace, built in the 19th century by the Pasha El Glaoui, is a gem of Islamic architecture. Tours are given daily. The Garden Agdal consists of a beautiful man-made lake surrounded by olive orchards. Housed here is a hundred-year-old boat that was used by the Black Sultan.

Other fascinating places are:

The Museum of Moroccan Arts, featuring costumes, textiles, jewelry and artifacts.

The dyers' souks, where wools, cottons and silks are dyed every imaginable color and hung in the sun to dry.

The leather tanneries, interesting but rather smelly; they are worth a visit.

The Al Mouasin Fountain, with elaborate mosaics.

The Menara Gardens, where sultans walked amidst the cypress groves.

The Bab Doukkala Gate, the site of the morning produce market.

The Ali Ibn Youssef Mosque.

The Royal Palace.

Marrakech

Marrakech a jouit de plusieurs noms non officiels mais bien mérités au cours des années, tels que "la Perle du Sud" et "la Ville des délices terrestres."

Marrakech fut fondé à l'onzième siècle par le chef des Berbères Almoravides, Abou Bekr. Enrichi de butin provenant d'un raid dans l'Espagne, Marrakech fut le centre commercial du Maroc durant les dernières années du onzième siècle.

Marrakech est la Grande Ville des Berbères, et a réussi à préserver la structure médiévale pure qui y existait au moment de sa fondation.

Aujourd'hui, Marrakech est une ville culturelle florissante et pleine d'activité où prédomine le tourisme. La ville se divise en deux sections: la vieille ville, ou médine, où des multitudes de piétons encombrent les ruelles qui serpentent à travers les marchés, tout comme ils l'ont fait depuis des siècles; et la nouvelle ville, appelée Guéliz, où les Français ont laissé leur empreinte. Là, les rues sont larges, et des cafés modernes sur les trottoirs servent des mets du monde entier; banques, offices de tourisme, libraires, agences de compagnies aériennes: vous trouverez tous les conforts du 20ème siecle à Guéliz.

Les deux villes, qui sont séparées d'un kilomètre et demi, sont reliées par l'avenue Mohammed V. C'est sur cette avenue au centre de Guéliz que vous trouverez l'office de tourisme.

Le minaret de la Koutoubia (Souvenez-vous que les non-musulmans ne sont pas admis et que les appareils photo sont interdits.) Cette mosquée marocaine des plus vénérées est le meilleur point de départ pour votre visite. Le nom "Koutoubia" est dérivé du mot arabe "kutubbiyyin" qui signifie "livre" ou "bibliothèque." Cette mosquée a toujours été reliée à une bibliothèque, et abritait autrefois une copie du Coran que le Sultan mérinide Abu Al-Mumim avait rapportée de Cordoba. Cette copie avait appartenu à Uthman Ibn Affan, le troisième caliphe orthodoxe, et contenait quatre prières écrites de sa propre main, mais elle fut perdu en mer au 13ème siècle. *(p. 192)*

La place Jemaa-el-Fna (assemblée des morts) est l'attraction touristique la plus connue de Marrakech, et pour bonne raison. La Jemaa-el-Fna est un immense espace ouvert à l'entrée de la médine. Ici se rassemblent des conteurs, danseurs, et acrobates, charmeurs de serpents et avaleurs de feu, devins, sorciers, et animaux savants, jouant tous pour des pièces de monnaie comme cela s'est fait depuis des siècles. Ne perdez pas votre portefeuille de vue, mais amusez-vous bien au spectacle.

Les Tombeaux saâdiens furent bâtis par Ahmed Al Mansour en 1578 comme cimetière pour la famille royale saâdienne. Ils furent emmurés vers 1700 par Moulay Ismail et redécouverts 200 ans plus tard, en 1911. Soixante-deux sultans, leurs femmes et leurs enfants furent enterrés ici, et il y a cent tombeaux de plus dans la cour.

Le Palais de la Bahia, construit au 19ème siècle par le Pasha El Glaoui, est un joyau d'architecture islamique. On offre des tours du palais tous les jours. Le Jardin Agdal consiste en un beau lac artificiel entouré de vergers d'oliviers. On préserve ici un bâteau datant d'il y a cent ans que le sultan noir avait utilisé.

Et voici d'autres endroits fascinants à visiter:

Le Musée d'Arts marocains, qui exhibe des costumes, textiles, bijoux et objets fabriqués.

Les souks des teinturiers, où la laine, le coton, et la soie sont teints en toutes les couleurs imaginables, et pendus au soleil pour sécher.

Les tanneries de cuir, intéressantes mais un peu puantes; elles méritent une visite.

La Fontaine Al Mouasin, avec des mosaïques élaborées.

Les Jardins Menara, où les sultans se réunissaient parmi les bosquets de cyprès.

La Porte Bab Doukkala, le site du marché matinal de produits maraîchers.

La mosquée d'Ali Ibn Youssef.

Le palais royal.

La Mosquée de Sidi Bel Abbes.

Photo: Hahn

Fish market, Marrakesh.
Marché au poisson, Marrakech.

Photo: Bertrand, Marrakesh

Blue people of the Sahara.
Touaregs du Sahara.

Cities, Villages and other places of Interest, A Listing

Agadir—Located on the Atlantic, 240 km from Marrakesh, Agadir is a very important sea resort. It claims the longest beach in all of Morocco, a crescent shape 10 km long and 365 m wide. Agadir is at the foot of an impressive cliff, topped by an imposing 16th Century citadel which was restored in the 18th Century. One of the most attractive features of Agadir is its Kasbah, perched 236 meters above sea level. You'll find excellent leather shops, good restaurants and hotels, and plenty of night life here.

Amtoudi—The very last leg of the southern excursion to the Sahara, on the back of a donkey. The rocky formations are impressive.

Asilah—45 km south of Tangiers on the shore of the Mediterranean. A fishing port with an impressive Kasbah. Several small seaside restaurants outside the town walls serve the daily catch to passers-by.

Azrou—Built on a hillside in a cedar forest, Azrou is a mountain village 67 km from Meknes. The House of Craftsmanship (Maison de l'Artisanat) is a must-see for tourists.

Chaouen—120 km from Tangiers and high in the Rif Mountains. This is a beautiful Spanish/Moroccan town, a perfect blending in architecture and style. There are steep green foothills covered with orchards and pastures, and quaint tin-roofed houses.

El Jadida—This coastal fortress city, which was ruled by the Portuguese for centuries beginning in 1502, is especially interesting to visit. The spacious underground room which is part of the old fortress is a remarkable piece of engineering.

Essaouria—75 km from Marrakesh on the Atlantic coast. The name means "small fortress surrounded by walls." Essaouria was formerly called Mogador. Remains of pottery found on the islands in the bay testify to the presence of Phoenicians in the region from the 6th and 7th Centuries

"Blue People Visiting the Souk," mixed media by Marcyne Johnson, Tucson, Arizona.
"Touaregs visitant le souk," divers matériaux, par Marcyne Johnson, Tucson, Arizona.

Villes, villages et autres sites intéressants: une liste

Agadir—*A 240 km de Marrakech, c'est une station balnéaire très importante. Agadir possède la plage la plus longue du Maroc; en forme de croissant, elle est 10 km de long et 365 m de large. Agadir se trouve au pied d'un escarpement impressionnant couronné d'une citadelle imposante du 16ème siècle, restaurée au 18ème siècle. Une des plus séduisantes attractions d'Agadir est sa Kasbah, perchée à 236 m au-dessus du niveau de la mer. Vous y trouverez d'excellentes boutiques de maroquinerie, de bons restaurants et hôtels, et une abondance de vie nocturne.*

Amtoudi—*C'est la toute dernière étape de l'excursion méridionale au Sahara à dos d'âne. Il y a là des magnifiques formations rocheuses.*

Asilah—*A 45 km au sud de Tanger sur la côte de la Méditerranée, c'est un port de pêche avec une kasbah frappante. Plusieurs petits restaurants au bord de la mer en dehors de la ville servent la prise du jour aux passants.*

Azrou—*Bâti sur un coteau dans une forêt de cèdres, Azrou est un village de mountagne à 67 km de Meknès. Les touristes doivent absolument y visiter la Maison de l'Artisanat!*

Chaouen—*120 km de Tanger et très haut dans les montagnes du Rif, c'est une belle ville espagnole/marocaine, une fusion parfaite de ces architectures et styles; les contreforts verdoyants escarpés sont couverts de vergers et pâturages et on y retrouve des pittoresques maisons à toits de fer blanc.*

B.C. onwards. Spain, Portugal and England vied with Moroccan pirates for control of the coast. Essaouria has a beautiful beach and an active fishing port. Inlaid wood crafts are available here.

Goulimine—200 km from Agadir, at the edge of the Sahara. Saturday is camel market day. You'll see the "Blue Men" in their voluminous blue dyed garments. Next stop is Timbuktu, if you're up for it.

Ifrane—This village specializes in winter sports and is just 71 km from Meknes. Watch for a beautiful palace high on a hill in Ifrane. It resembles a storybook palace.

Inezgane—Just a few miles from Agadir, with a densely crowded and authentic market for bargain shoppers: mainly tooled leather, slippers, and various kinds of Moroccan souvenirs.

Lixus—38 km from Asilah and one of the oldest cities in Morocco. Lixus was a Phoenician trading post as early as the 6th Century B.C. Remains of the temples, baths, and theatre make up the acropolis at the top of the hill.

Ouarzazate—215 km south of Marrakesh and the threshold of the South Sahara. You'll drive over a 7,400 ft pass to the Draa Valley. Ouarzazate is a fortified city of earthen tones, with towers that appear unchanged since Biblical times.

Oukaimeden—A popular winter sports resort boasting Africa's highest ski chair lifts.

Ourika Valley—A quaint Berber village just an hour's drive from Marrakesh, past lush fields and orchards along the river. This is a pleasant stop on the way up the mountain to Oukaimeden.

Safi—A busy port which was once a Phoenician trading post. Now it is an exporter of phosphates and has an annual production of ninety thousand tons of sardines. Safi is one of the main sources for pottery in Morocco.

Tafraoute—A delightful village surrounded by palm trees and famed for its almonds. This village is situated in the west of the Anti Atlas, between Agadir and Tiznit. The excursion to Tafraoute is most interesting. The best time to go is February, Almond Festival time.

Tangiers—As the gateway between Europe and Africa, in Tangiers the European influence is apparent. Moulay Ismail chose the Kasbah of Tangiers as the ideal place to build his palace. Visit the Museum of Moroccan Art, the Sultan's Gardens and the Antiquities Museum.

Taroudant—80 km from Agadir and the center of the Sous region. Gigantic fortifications have been kept in good repair and the area is covered with olive groves, citrus orchards and lush green fields.

Tiznit—92 km from Agadir is this fortified desert oasis. The souks carry the heavy old Berber jewelry and the decoratively encrusted weapons of Morocco. Many interesting excursions can be made from Tiznit to the Anti Altas and Foum el Hassan, Akka, Tata and Foum Zguid.

Volubilis—30 km from Meknes, archeological digs on the site of the Roman ruins of Volubilis, which was destroyed by the earthquake in 1755, brought to light a whole polygonal city spread over 40 acres. You'll see the forum, basilica, precinct, triumphal arch, palace, houses, thermal baths, aqueducts, and streets.

Rupestine Stations of Morocco—where you can find cave paintings of antelopes, ostriches, elephants and other animals.

The rams of Tarraga near Figuig.

The elephants of Tamegoul and Merkala.

The Bestiary of Taourirt.

The Great Necropolis of Erfoud.

Foum El Hassan is a very important station. The cave paintings found there date back as far as 500 to 2000 B.C.

El Jadida—*Cette ville-forteresse côtière, autrefois gouvernée par les Portuguais dès 1502, est particuilèrement intéressante à visiter. La spacieuse salle souterraine qui fait partie de la vieille forteresse est une oeuvre d'ingénierie remarquable.*

Essaouria—*Situé à 75 km de Marrakech sur la côte de l'Atlantique, Essaouria, dont le nom signifie "petite forteresse cernée de murs," s'appelait Mogador autrefois. Des tissons de poterie retrouvés sur les îles dans la baie attestent la présence des Phéniciens dans la région depuis les 6ème et 7ème siècles av. J.-C. L'Espagne, le Portugal et l'Angleterre ont lutté avec les pirates marocains pour contrôler sa côte. Essaouria a une ravissante plage et un port de pêche actif. Des articles de marqueterie sont disponibles ici.*

Goulimine—*Situé à 200 km d'Agadir, au bord du Sahara. Samedi, c'est le jour du marché de chameaux. Vous verez les "Hommes bleus" dans leurs vêtements volumineux teints en bleu. Le prochain arrêt sera Tombouktou, si vous vous sentez d'attaque à y aller.*

Ifrane—*Ce village se spécialise en sports d'hiver; il n'est qu'à 71 km de Meknès. Cherchez de vue un beau palais très haut sur une colline à Ifrane. Il rappelle un château dans un conte.*

Inezgane—*Rien qu'à quelques kilomètres d'Agadir, cette ville a un marché authentique très encombré pour les chercheurs d'occasions; on y vend principalement du cuir repoussé, des pantoufles, et diverses sortes de souvenirs marocains.*

Lixus—*A 38 km d'Asilah, c'est une des plus anciennes villes du Maroc. Lixus avait été un centre commercial phénicien dès le 6ème siècle av. J.-C. Des vestiges de temples, de bains, et d'un théatre forment l'acropole au sommet de la colline.*

Ouarzazate—*A 215 km au sud de Marrakech, c'est le seuil du Sahara méridional. Vous traverserez un col de 2255 m de hauteur pour arriver à la vallée du Draa. Ouarzazate est une ville fortifiée, en couleurs de terre, avec des tours qui semblent inchangées depuis les temps bibliques.*

Oukaimeden—*C'est une station de sports d'hiver populaire qui est fière d'avoir les télésièges les plus hauts de l'Afrique.*

Vallée d'Ourika—*Un village berbère pittoresque, à peine à une heure de route de Marrakech, en passant par des champs et vergers riches le long du fleuve. C'est un arrêt agréable quand on monte la montagne vers Oukaimeden.*

Safi—*Un port très actif qui était autrefois un centre commercial phénicien, Safi est maintenant un exportateur de phosphates et a une production annuelle de 90.000 tonnes de sardines. Safi est une des principales sources de poterie du Maroc.*

Tafraoute—*Un village ravissant entouré de palmiers et renommé pour ses amandes. Ce village est situé à l'ouest de l'Anti Atlas, entre Agadir et Tiznit. L'excursion à Tafraoute est des plus intéressantes. Le meilleur moment d'y aller c'est en février, au moment de la Fête des Amandes.*

Tanger—*Le point où l'Afrique et l'Europe se rencontrent, dans cette ville cosmopolite l'influence européenne est apparente. Moulay Ismail avait choisi la Kasbah de Tangers comme le lieu idéal pour bâtir son palais. Visitez le Musée d'Art marocain, les Jardins du Sultan et le Musée d'Antiquités.*

Taroudant—*A 80 km d'Agadir, c'est le centre de la région de Sous. Des fortifications gigantiques ont été bien entretenues et la région est couverte de bosquets d'oliviers, de vergers d'agrumes et de champs riches et verdoyants.*

Tiznit—*Cet oasis fortifié du désert se trouve à 92 km d'Agadir. Les souks vendent les vieux bijoux lourds berbères et les armes incrustées de façon décorative du Maroc. On peut faire beaucoup d'excursions intéressantes à partir de Tiznit à l'Anti Altas et à Foum el Hassan, Akka, Tata et Foum Zguid.*

Volubilis—*A 30 km de Meknès, les excavations archéologiques sur le site des ruines romaines de Volubilis, qui fut détruit par un tremblement de terre en 1755, on mis en lumière toute une ville polygonale étendue sur 40 acres. Vous verez le forum, la basilique, l'enceinte, l'arche triomphale, le palais, les maisons, les bains thermaux, les aqueducs et les rues.*

Stations rupestres du Maroc—*Vous pouvez y trouver des peintures rupestres d'antelopes, d'autruches, d'éléphants et d'autres animaux.*

Les béliers de Tarraga près de Figuig.

Les éléphants de Tamegoul et de Merkala.

Le Bestiaire de Taourirt.

La grande Nécropole d'Erfoud.

Foum El Hassan est une station très importante. Les peintures rupestres dans ces caves datent de 500 à 2.000 av. J.-C.

ASSISTANCE FROM WRITTEN SOURCES

It wouldn't be fair to limit you solely to my own knowledge of Morocco. There are many areas of the country that I'm not familiar with. Therefore, I have turned to various sources for information worth sharing. My thanks to *Lands and Peoples Encyclopedia, From the Far West: Carpets and Textiles of Morocco*, published by the Textile Museum, Washington, D.C., and *Vogue* Magazine. Various publications by the Moroccan Department of Tourism were also used. There are many worthwhile travel guides published on Morocco. Two which have helped me over the years are *Fodor's* and *Berlitz*. I thank them for their assistance, and I highly recommend them.

While on the subject of books, here is a tip on treasure hunting of another kind: do not overlook the Moroccan bookstores. They are filled with beautiful publications on travel, art, cooking and Moroccan treasures… many in French and English.

L'ASSISTANCE DES SOURCES ECRITES

Ce ne serait pas juste de vous limiter uniquement à mes propres connaissances du Maroc. Il y a plusieurs parties du pays que je ne connais pas. Je me suis donc tourné vers plusieurs sources pour des informations qui valent la peine d'être partagées. Je voudrais exprimer ma reconnaissance envers le Lands and Peoples Encyclopedia, De l'extrême Occident: tapis et textiles du Maroc, *publié par le Textile Museum, Washington, D.C., et le magazine* Vogue. *Nous avons aussi employé diverses publications du Département de Tourisme du Maroc. Il y a beaucoup de guides de voyage pour le Maroc qui méritent d'être lus; deux en particulier m'ont beaucoup aidé au cours des années:* Fodor et Berlitz. *Je les remercie de leur assistance, et je les recommande vivement.*

Et en ce qui concerne les livres, voici une suggestion sur une chasse aux trésor de type différent: ne négligez pas les librairies marocaines. Elles sont pleines de belles publications sur les voyages, les arts, la cuisine et les trésors marocains…et beaucoup sont en français et en anglais.

Photo: Author

Mogador

Mogador Island Prison, built by the Portuguese in the 18th Century, is a historical landmark. The prison site is now a monument to the past and can only be visited by special permission. I would like to thank the authorities in Essaouira for that special permission.

Mogador

La Prison de l'Ile de Mogador, construite par les Portuguais au 18ème siècle, est un site historique et un monument qui commémore le passé. On ne peut pas la visiter sans permission spéciale. Je voudrais donc remercier les autorités à Essaouira de m'avoir accordé cette permission spéciale.

Photo: Author

Mogador Prison: The central courtyard and mosque.
Prison de Mogador: la cour centrale et la mosquée.

Photo: Author

Walls twenty feet high and two feet thick house the four doors to the courtyard.
Les quatres portes donnant à la cour sont situées dans des murs de vingt pieds de haut et de deux pieds de large.

Photo: Island caretaker

The single entrance to the prison courtyard as seen from the Minaret.
La seule entrée à la cour de la prison comme vue du minaret.

Photo: Author

The solitary well inside the courtyard, rumored to have been an escape route.
L'unique puits dans la cour: on dit que ce fut un chemin d'évasion.

Photo: Author

The Mosque of Mogador: Islam is for all Moslems.
La mosquée de Mogador: l'Islam est pour tous les Musulmans.

Photo: Island caretaker

Hand-sculptured passageway leading to the Minaret.
Passage taillé à la main, menant au minaret.

Photo: Author

Moorish architecture in stone dating back two centuries.
Architecture maure en pierre datant d'il y a deux siècles.

Photo: Author

Salt and sea air resculpt old masterpieces.
Le sel et l'air marin resculptent les vieux chefs-d'oeuvre.

Photo: Author

Small exits were fashioned from large doors.
Des petites sorties furent fabriquées dans les grandes portes.

Photo: Author

Rusty cannons that once threatened unwelcome visitors.
Des canons rouillés qui menaçaient autrefois les visiteurs importuns.

Photo: Author

Sea gulls act as Mogador's sentries today.
Les mouettes servent de guet pour Mogador aujourd'hui.

Photo: Author

Mogador is a protected breeding ground for the rare Eleanor's Falcon.
Mogador est un site de nidification protégé pour le rare faucon d'Eléonore.

Photo: Author

A lone caretaker watches a now deserted harbor.
Un gardien solitaire surveille un port maintenant désert.

Photo: Author

In the distance, the beautiful seaside town of Essaouira.
Au loin, la belle ville d'Essaouira au bord de la mer.

Photo: Author

A door in the Medina, Essaouira.
Une porte dans la médina, Essaouira.

The Berbers of Morocco

The Romans called these people "the Barbarians" because they defended their lands so vehemently. They call themselves the Imazghen (free people) because that is the way they have lived in Morocco since 3000 B.C.

Some speculate that the Berbers were descended from the Ancient Egyptians and Libyans. Others claim that they are from Southern Europe, and of Iberian stock. When the Arabs came in the 7th Century, they found these tribal people who were fiercely independent and committed to their own traditions. By the 8th Century, the Berbers had joined forces with the Arabs to conquer Spain.

Today, there are about 12 million Berbers in Morocco, belonging to about 600 different tribes. Many have mixed with Arabs, both genetically and culturally, and for the most part the two groups are broken down into "Berber-speaking" and "Arab-speaking" sub-groups.

Most Berbers depend on raising livestock and farming for a living. They live in compact villages, often in rugged mountain areas. Some are pastoral, moving from the desert to the mountains in the summer for better grazing. Other Berber-speaking groups, such as the Tuaregs of the Sahara, roam the desert with herds of camels, cattle, goats and sheep. The indigo traditionally used to dye their voluminous garments tints their skin blue, and this is why they are called the "Blue Men of the Sahara."

My personal contact with the rural Arab Berbers has been confined to country marketplaces and a few mountain villages off the beaten path, during my travels in search of rugs. I have found the people to be shy with strangers, but warm and friendly after the slightest introduction.

Les Berbères du Maroc

Les Romains avaient nommé ce peuple "les Barbares" parce qu'ils défendaient leurs terres avec tant de violence. En langue berbère, ils s'appellent les Imazghen (peuple libre) puisque c'est ainsi qu'ils ont vécu au Maroc depuis 3000 av. J.-C.

Certains savants pensent que les Berbères sont issus des ancients Egyptiens et Libyens. D'autres prétendent qu'ils proviennent de l'Europe méridionale et qu'ils sont d'origine ibérienne. Quand les Arabes arriverent au 7ème siecle, ils rencontrèrent ces peuples tribaux ardemment indépendants et dévoués à leurs propres traditions. Dès le 8ème siècle, les Berbères s'étaient joints aux Arabes pour conquérir l'Espagne.

Aujourd'hui il y a environ 12 millions de Berbères au Maroc, appartenant à environ 600 tribus différentes. Beaucoup se sont entremelés avec les Arabes, génétiquement et culturellement, et en général les deux groupes sont divisés en "groupes qui parlent le berbère" et "groupes qui parlent l'arabe."

La plupart des Berbères vivent de l'élevage et de l'agriculture. Ils habitent des villages compacts situés souvent dans des régions montagneuses accidentées. Certains sont pastoraux, menant leurs troupeaux du désert aux montagnes pendant l'été pour retrouver les meilleurs pâturages. D'autres groupes qui parlent la langue berbère, tels que les Touaregs du Sahara, parcourent le désert avec des troupeaux de chameaux, bovins, chèvres et moutons. L'indigo qu'ils utilisent traditionnellement pour teindre leurs vetêments volumineux teint leur peau en bleu aussi, et c'est pour cela qu'on les appelle les "Hommes bleus du Sahara."

Mon contact personnel avec les Berbères arabes s'est limité aux marchés ruraux et villages reculés que j'ai visités à la recherche de tapis. J'ai trouvé que ces gens sont timides avec les inconnus, mais qu'ils sont gentils et amicaux avec ceux dont ils ont fait la moindre connaissance.

The Berbers of Morocco. *Les Berbères du Maroc.*

Photo: Author

Hajjam Boubker and wife, Fatima: Berbers of Tiflet.
Hajjam Boubker et son épouse, Fatima: Berbères de Tiflet.

Photo: Gingrich

Turn of the century bronze Moroccan horseman, 600 lbs. AMMA.
Cavalier marocain en bronze du début du siècle, 600 livres. AMMA.

Fantasias, moussems, parades, races, horse shows: anytime is an occasion for Moroccans to demonstrate their equestrian talents and their splendid horses.

Aux moussems, fantasias, courses, parades, concours hippiques: les Marocains saisissent toute occasion pour exposer leurs talents équestres et leurs chevaux splendides.

Fairs and Festivals of Morocco

Many dates vary from year to year. Contact one of the Moroccan Tourist Offices listed for exact dates and specific information.

January:

None listed officially; however, in Morocco you may see a Fantasia at any time.

February:

1. Almond Festival in Tafraout
2. Wax Lantern Festival in Salé

March:

1. Theater Festival in Casablanca

April:

1. The International Fair in Casablanca (every two years)
2. Festival of African Popular Arts in Agadir
3. Honey Festival in Immouzer des Ida ou Tanane (near Agadir)

May and June:

1. Regional Fair in Meknes
2. Festival of Roses in Kelaa des M'Gouna (near Ouarzazate)
3. Clementine Festival in Berkane (near Oujda)
4. National Folklore Festival in Marrakesh
5. Cherry Festival in Sefrou (near Fez)
6. Regional Fair in Fez

July:

1. Youth Festival (Fête de la Jeunesse)
2. Sea Festival in Al Hoceima
3. Orange Festival in Agadir
4. Week of Popular Mediterranean Arts in Tangier
5. Regional Fair in Taza and Tetouan

August:

1. Pear and Apple Festival in Immouzer du Kandar (near Fez)
2. Cultural Festival in Asilah

September:

1. Arab Theater Festival in Rabat
2. Fantasia Festival in Meknes
3. Bridal Festival in Imilchil (third week in September)
4. Snow Festival in Mischliffen

October:

1. Horse Festival in Tissa (near Fez)
2. Date Festival in Esrashidia and Erfoud
3. Festival of Traditional Arts in Fez

Fêtes et festivals du Maroc

Beaucoup de dates varient d'une année à l'autre. Adressez-vous à un des Offices Nationaux Marocains du Tourisme énumérés pour les dates exactes et des informations spécifiques.

Janvier:

Il n'y a pas de fêtes ou festivals sur la liste officielle en janvier, mais au Maroc on peut assister à des fantasias pendant toute l'année.

Février:

1. *Fête des amandiers en fleurs à Tafraout*
2. *Fête des lanternes de cire à Salé*

Mars:

1. *Festival de Théatre à Casablanca*

Avril:

1. *Rencontre internationale à Casablanca (tous les deux ans)*
2. *Rencontre des Arts Populaires africains d'Agadir*
3. *Fête du miel à Immouzer des Ida ou Tanane (près d'Agadir)*

Mai et juin:

1. *Festival régional à Meknès*
2. *Fête des roses à Kelaa des M'Gouna (près d'Ouarzazate)*
3. *Fête des clémentines à Berkane (près d'Oujda)*
4. *Festival national des Arts populaires à Marrakech*
5. *Fête des cerises à Séfrou (près de Fès)*
6. *Festival régional de Fès*

Juillet:

1. *Fête de la Jeunesse*
2. *Fête maritime à Al Hoceima*
3. *Fête des oranges à Agadir*
4. *Semaine des Arts méditerannéens populaires à Tanger*
5. *Festivals régionaux à Taza et Tétouan*

Août:

1. *La Fête des poires et des pommes à Immouzer du Kandar (près de Fès)*
2. *Festival culturel à Asilah*

Septembre:

1. *Festival du Théatre arabe à Rabat*
2. *Festival de Fantasias à Meknès*
3. *Moussem des fiancés à Imilchil (troisième semaine de septembre)*
4. *Fête des neiges à Mischliffen*

Octobre:

1. *Fête du cheval à Tissa (près de Fès)*

Photo: Hahn

Moroccan horseman preparing for the Fantasia. Fez.
Cavalier marocain se préparant pour la fantasia. Fès.

Photo: Hahn

Moroccan horsemen discussing the charge. Fez.
Cavaliers marocains discutant la charge. Fès.

November:
1. Regional Fair in Marrakesh

December:
1. Tangerine Festival in Berkane
2. Olive Festival in Rafai (near Fez)

2. Fète des dattes à Esrashidia et Erfoud
3. Festival des Arts traditionnels à Fès

Novembre:
1. Festival régional à Marrakech

Décembre:
1. Fête des mandarines à Berkane
2. Fête des olives à Rafai (près de Fès)

Religious Festivals:

Moussems / *Fêtes religieuses: Moussems*
(Dates may vary month to month. /
Les dates peuvent varier d'un mois à l'autre.)

May and June / *mai et juin:*
Sidi M'Hamed Benamar: Goulimine
Sidi Moussa: Casablanca
Sidi Magdoul: Essaouria
Moulay Bouselham: Kenitra

July / *juillet:*
Outa Hammon: Chaouen

August / *août:*
Sidi Lacheen: Temara (near Rabat/*près de Rabat*)
Dar Zhirou: Rabat
Sitti Fatma: Ourika (near Marrakesh/*près de Marrakech*)
Sidi Magdoul: Essaouria
Sidi Ali ou Moussa: Tiznit
Moulay Driss: Zerhoun

September / *septembre:*
Sidi Ahmed el Bernousir: Fez
Sidi Abdalhak ben Yasin: Marrakesh
El Guern: Marrakesh
Sidi Bonatinane: Marrakesh
Moulay Idriss Zerhoun: Moulay Idriss (near Meknes/*près de Meknès*)
Ait Baha: Agadir
Moulay Abdallah: El Jadida

Photo: Hahn

Moroccan horseman and horse, eager for the event. Fez.
Cavalier et cheval marocains, impatients d'assister à l'événement. Fès.

Fantasia: The Charge. Fez. *Fantasia: la charge. Fès.* Photo: Hahn

Sidi Yahia: Oujda
None in October, November & December /
Aucune en octobre, novembre et décembre

National Holidays

Moharrem 1 (Moslem New Year's Day)
Moharrem 10 Achoura (New Year Festival)
April:
Mouloud (Birthday of Prophet)
Ramadan: 30 day fast
Id el-Fitr: "The Lesser Festival" end of Ramadan
Id el-Adha: "The Greater Festival" Abraham's unfinished sacrifice
March 3: Fête du Trône (Accession of King Hassan II)
May 23: National Holiday
July 9: Fête de la Jeunesse (youth festival)
August 14: The Oued Eddahab Allegiance Day
August 20: The King and the People's Revolution Day
November 6: Green March Anniversary
November 18: Independence Day (Triumphal Return of Mohammed V)

Fêtes nationales

Moharrem 1 (premier jour de l'an musulman)
Moharrem 10 Achoura (Fête du nouvel an)
Avril:
Mouloud (Anniversaire du Prophète)
Ramadan: jeûne de 30 jours
Id el-Fitr: "la petite fête" à la fin du Ramadan
Id el-Adha: "la grande fête" commémorant le sacrifice inachevé d'Abraham
3 mars: *Fête du Trône (l'Accession du Roi Hassan II)*
23 mai: *Fête nationale*
9 juillet: *Fête de la Jeunesse*
14 août: *Jour de l'Allégeance de l'Oued Eddahab*
20 août: *Jour du Roi et de la Révolution du Peuple*
6 novembre: *Anniversaire de la Marche Verte*
18 novembre: *Jour de l'Indépendance du Maroc (Retour triomphal de Feu S.M. Mohammed V)*

The Souks

The souk is one of the most characteristic aspects of rural life. It's a place and a means of traditional trade. Since the Moroccan population is rural, each tribe has a certain number of souks that are generally held outside, or inside a special enclosing wall. These souks usually carry the name of the day on which they are held.

Les souks

Le souk est un des aspects les plus caractéristiques de la vie rurale. C'est un lieu où se fait le commerce national, et un moyen de le faire. Puisque la population marocaine est largement rurale, chaque tribu a un certain nombre de souks qui sont tenus dehors, ou à l'intérieur d'une enceinte spéciale. On donne à ces souks le nom du jour de la semaine qu'ils sont tenus.

THE MAIN SOUKS OF MOROCCO
LES PRINCIPAUX SOUKS DU MAROC

Place	Days/*jours*
PROVINCE: AGADIR	
AGADIR	Sat-Sun/*samedi-dimanche*
INEZGAN	Tues/*mardi*
TAROUDANT	Fri/*vendredi*
PROVINCE: SHEFSHAOUEN	
SHEFSHAOUEN	Thurs/*jeudi*
PROVINCE: ERRACHIDIA (KSAR-ES-SOUK)	
ERFOUD	Sun/*dimanche*
ERRACHIDIA	Sun-Tues-Thurs/ *dimanche-mardi-jeudi*
RISSANI	Sun-Tues-Thurs/ *dimanche-mardi-jeudi*
PROVINCE: KHEMISSET	
KHEMISSET	Tues/*mardi*
TIFLET	Wed/*mercredi*
PROVINCE: KHENIFRA	
MIDELT	Sun/*dimanche*
PROVINCE: KENITRA	
SIDI ALLAL BAHRAOUI	Sun/*dimanche*
SOUK SEBT OF KENITRA	Sat/*samedi*
SOUK HAD OULED JELLOUL	Sun/*dimanche*
SOUK TLETA	Tues/*mardi*
SOUK EL ARBA	Wed/*mercredi*
SOUK KHMIS RMILA	Thurs/*jeudi*
JAMAA MOGRAN	Fri/*vendredi*
JAMAA LALLA MIMOUNA	Fri/*vendredi*
HAD KAMOUNI	Sun/*dimanche*

Place	Days/*jours*
PROVINCE: MARRAKECH	
MARRAKECH	Thurs/*jeudi* (Souk of camels/*de chameaux*)
SIDI EL'AIDI	Thurs/*jeudi*
PROVINCE: OUARZAZATE	
OUARZAZATE	Sun/*dimanche*
SKOURA	Mon-Thurs/*lundi-jeudi*
TAZNAKHTE	Sun/*dimanche*
TALIOUIN	Mon/*lundi*
ASKAOUN	Thurs/*jeudi*
ZAGOURA	Wed-Thurs/*mercredi-jeudi*
AGDZ	Thurs/*jeudi*
BAGOUMITE	Thurs-Sun/*jeudi-dimanche*
M'HAMID	Mon/*lundi*
BOUMALN	Wed/*mercredi*
TINERHIR	Mon/*lundi*
EL KALAA	Wed/*mercredi*
PROVINCE: TIZNIT	
BOU-IZAKARN	Fri/*vendredi*
GOULMINA	Sat/*samedi* (Souk of camels/*de chameaux*)
TIZNIT	Thurs-Fri/*jeudi-vendredi*

Photo: Hahn

Information courtesy of Moroccan National Tourist Office, Rabat.
Ces informations proviennent l'Office National Marocain de Tourisme, à Rabat.

Photo: Sisk

"Man of the Countryside," watercolor, by Joseph Bohler, Colorado.
"Homme de la campagne," aquarelle, par Joseph Bohler, Colorado.

The Taylors with a rug merchant, marketplace of Khemisset. Photo: J. Bircher
Les Taylors avec un marchand de tapis, marché de Khemisset.

Most of all, have a good time!

When my plane lands in Casablanca, it is usually filled with three categories of passengers: Moroccans returning home, people coming to Morocco on business, and scores of tourists who have come for that wonderful three letter word—FUN—in which case there is no better place for them to go. Besides an unbeatable year-round climate, Morocco has hundreds of miles of white sandy beaches on two different coastlines; breathtaking mountains rising fourteen thousand feet above the Sahara Desert; a culture boasting more than two thousand years of recorded history; and beautiful things to buy, as this book will show you.

So try on costumes, taste new foods, go on day trips to the country markets, ride a camel, meet people, make memories. . .The experience is out there waiting, and it's all up to you!

Most of all, have a good time!

Avant tout, amusez-vous bien!

Quand mon avion attérit à Casablanca, il est d'habitude rempli de trois catégories de passagers: des Marocains qui rentrent chez eux, des gens qui viennent au Maroc pour faire des affaires, et un grand nombre de touristes qui viennent pour s'amuser: dans ce cas-là, ils sont venus au meilleur endroit possible. Outre un climat sans égal pendant toute l'année, le Maroc possède des centaines de kilomètres de plages blanches sableuses sur deux littoraux différents; des montagnes stupéfiantes qui s'élèvent à quatre mille deux cents mètres au-dessus du désert du Sahara; une culture qui est fière d'avoir plus de deux mille ans d'histoire écrite; et des belles choses à acheter, comme ce livre va vous montrer.

Alors essayez les costumes, goûtez aux nouveaux aliments, faites des excursions d'une journée aux marchés ruraux, promenez-vous à dos d'un chameau, recueillez des souvenirs...l'expérience vous attend là, c'est à vous d'en jouir!

Avant tout, amusez-vous bien!

Photo: J. Taylor

Berber weaver with a woven pillow cover, marketplace of Khemisset.
Tisseuse berbère avec une taie de coussin tissée, marché de Khemisset.

Photo: Hahn

Vegetable market, Middle Atlas Mountains.
Marché aux légumes, Moyen Atlas.

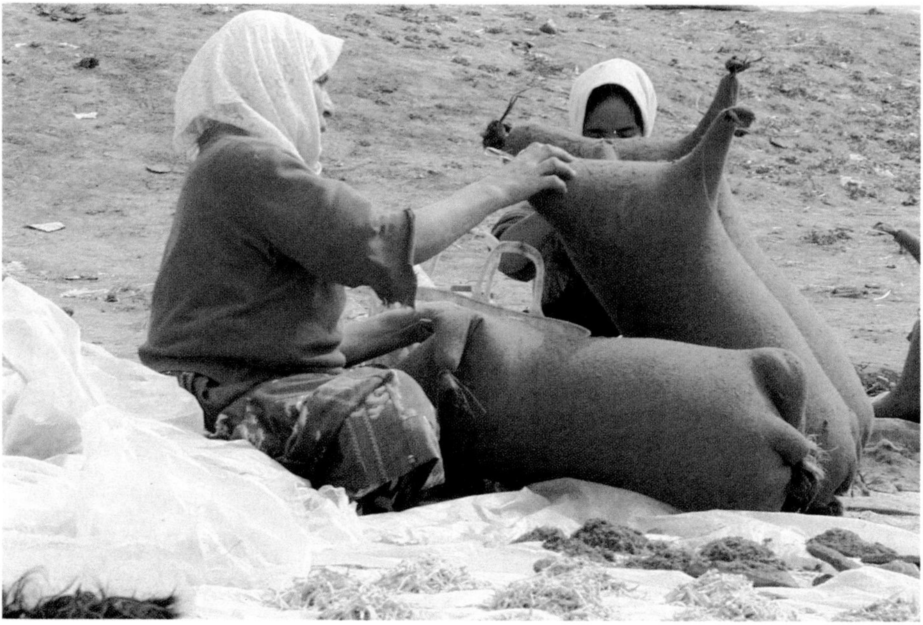

Photo: Walker

Tanning goatskin waterbags, Middle Atlas Mountains.
Tannage d'outres d'eau en peau de bouc, Moyen Atlas.

Photo: Author

Rug market, Middle Atlas Mountains.
Marché de tapis, Moyen Atlas.

Photo: : Hahn

Typical bus used for AMMA Moroccan tours, Chellah Gardens, Rabat.
Bus typique, utilisé pour les tours du Maroc de l'AMMA, Jardins de Chellah, Rabat.

Photo: Author

Judi Taylor in the hotel Palais Jamai, Fez.
Judi Taylor à l'hôtel Palais Jamai, Fès.

Transportation, Accommodations and Guide Service

Here's a pre-departure tip that I hope you will use but never need: write down your passport, traveler's check and airline ticket numbers. Put them in a safe place or exchange them with a fellow traveler. In case of loss, this will minimize your inconvenience.

Royal Air Maroc Airlines is Morocco's major airline company and offers excellent service to and from Europe and the United States. Most flights are routed through Casablanca's Mohammed V Airport. When leaving Morocco, allow yourself at least an extra hour. The airport is extremely busy.

Transport, logement et service de guide

Voici un conseil avant votre départ; j'espère que vous le suivrez mais que vous n'en aurez jamais besoin: notez vos numéros de passport, de chèques de voyage et de billets d'avion. Gardez-les dans un lieu sûr ou échangez-les avec ceux d'un compagnon de voyage. Ceci diminuera les inconvénients en cas de perte.

Le Royal Air Maroc est la compagnie aérienne principale du Maroc et elle offre des services excellents dans les deux sens de l'Europe et des Etats-Unis. La plupart des vols passent par l'Aéroport Mohammed V de Casablanca. En quittant le Maroc, il faut compter sur une heure de plus pour s'embarquer, car l'aéroport est grouillant d'activité.

LIST OF ROYAL AIR MAROC AGENCIES IN MOROCCO
LISTE D'AGENCES DU ROYAL AIR MAROC AU MAROC

CITY/*VILLE*	ADDRESS/*ADRESSE*	TELEPHONE
AGADIR	Av. Général Kettani	231-45 / 46 (08)
AL HOCEIMA	Aéroport Côte du Rif	20.05 & 20.06 (98)
CASABLANCA	44, Place Mohammed V 44, Av. des F.A.R. & 22.41.41 (0)	27.11.22 & 27.32.11
FEZ	54, Av. Hassan II	255.16 & 17 (06)
MARRAKESH	197, Av. Mohammed V & 309.39 (04)	319-38 & 39 - 301.38
MEKNES	7. Av. Mohammed V	209.63 & 64 (05)
OUJDA	Bd. Mohammed V	39.63/64 - 39.09 (068)
RABAT	Angle Av. Mohammed V et Rue Al Amir Moulay Abdallah	697.10 / 680.76 (07)
TANGIER/*TANGER*	Place de France	347-22 (09)
TETOUAN	5, Av. Mohammed V	20.60 / 65.77 (096)
DAKHLA	Av. des P.T.T. B.P. 191	49
LAAYOUNE	7, Place Bir Anzarane	22.40.71/77
NADOR	Angle Bd. Mohammed V	38.46/23.37 (060)
OURAZAZATE	Aéroport Taourirte	146.148
TAN-TAN	Avenue de la Ligue Arabe	

Information courtesy of Moroccan National Tourist Office, Rabat.
Ces informations proviennent de l'Office National Marocain de Tourisme, à Rabat.

Morocco has good highways, and rental cars are available. Fuel is expensive. The bus network in Morocco is complete and will take you to even the most remote areas of the country. The C.T.M. is the government bus company; it maintains strong equipment and tight schedules. The smaller, independent companies are more crowded, but cheap and efficient.

Trains run north and south between most major cities. They are quite modern on the whole and offer fast service and a good view of the countryside.

There are small (petit) taxis to take you around the major cities and large Mercedes (grand) taxis to chauffeur you between cities.

Morocco has many beautiful hotels with accommodations to fit every budget, from small, intimate rooms in the Medina (old city) to luxurious suites. It has three of the top ten hotels in the world: the Mamounia Hotel in Marrakesh, the Palais Jamai Hotel in Fez and the Hotel Gazelle d'Or in Taroudant.

Specific information on hotels can be obtained from the American Museum of Moroccan Art, Box 5047, Tucson, Arizona 85703-1472 (please enclose two dollars for postage and handling). If you know your travel dates, and would like some help with reservations, please enclose your telephone number (the return call from the AMMA will be collect).

Guides are available in Morocco through a government-monitored guide service. Official guides are usually designated by a badge. You will be approached repeatedly by young people claiming to be "students, not guides" who want to show you around. While I would not encourage you to break the rules by hiring one of the unofficial "student" guides, it is sometimes worth giving one of them a little money to keep the others away. Besides, any money you give them will be well spent.

Le Maroc a des bonnes routes nationales, et on peut louer y des voitures. L'essence coûte cher. Le réseau d'autobus au Maroc est complet et vous transportera même aux régions les plus éloignées du pays. La C.T.M. est la compagnie d'autobus gouvernementale; elle maintient des équipements solides et des horaires serrés. Les compagnies indépendantes plus petites sont plus bondées, mais aussi meilleur marché et efficaces.

Les trains font le service nord-sud entre la plupart des villes principales. Ils sont bien modernes en général et ils offrent du service rapide et une bonne vue de la campagne.

Il y a des petits taxis qui vous conduiront autour des villes principales, et des grands taxis Mercedes qui vous prendront d'une ville à l'autre.

Le Maroc a beaucoup de beaux hôtels et des logements pour tous les budgets, des petites chambres intimes dans la médine (la vieille ville) jusqu'aux grandes suites luxueuses. Ce pays contient trois des dix meilleurs hôtels du monde: l'Hôtel Mamounia à Marrakech, l'Hôtel Palais Jamai à Fez et l'Hôtel Gazelle d'Or à Taroudant.

Vous pouvez obtenir des informations spécifiques sur les hôtels en écrivant à: American Museum of Moroccan Art, Box 50472, Tucson, Arizona, 85703-1422 USA (prière d'inclure deux dollars pour les tarifs postaux et de manutention). Si vous connaissez vos dates de voyage et voudriez qu'on vous aide à faire des réservations, nous vous prions de nous envoyer aussi votre numéro de téléphone (l'AMMA vous téléphonera en P.C.V.).

Des guides sont disponibles au Maroc par l'intermédiaire d'un service contrôlé par le gouvernement. Les guides officiels sont d'habitude désignés par un insigne. Vous serez approchés constamment par des jeunes gens prétendant être des "étudiants, pas des guides" qui voudront vous faire visiter le coin. Je ne voudrais pas vous encourager à violer la loi en embauchant un de ces guides "étudiants" non-nofficiels, mais ça vaut parfois la peine de donner un peu d'argent à un de ceux-ci pour que les autres vous laissent tranquilles. De toute manière, tout argent que vous leur donnez leur rendra bien service.

Clothing Tips and What to Expect of the Weather

Morocco is known for beautiful weather and clear skies. For the most part, light clothing will do, but the country does have mountainous cold weather (yes, they ski there) and Saharan temperature extremes, so it is a good idea to add a thick sweater or jacket to your wardrobe. The sun shines most of the time, so take a good sunblock.

Be sure to take good, soft-soled walking or running shoes. In the medinas, cars, carts, people and animals move along together at a slow steady pace on narrow streets, and you should be ready to step aside quickly!

Dress according to where you are. Around the beach towns or hotel pools, short shorts and skimpy attire are acceptable, while in the cities or rural areas it makes things much easier if you just cover yourself up a bit. Morocco is a Moslem country with rules of propriety that are different from ours. Although you are not required to behave like a Moslem, a little respect goes a long way.

Conseils sur l'habillement et prévisions météorologiques

Le Maroc est bien connu pour son beau temps et son ciel sans nuages. En général, des vêtements légers vous suffiront, mais ce pays connait aussi le froid des montagnes (oui, on fait du ski là-bas) et les températures extrêmes sahariennes, alors c'est une bonne idée d'inclure un chandail épais ou un veston dans votre garde-robe. Le soleil brille la plupart du temps: apportez donc une bonne crème solaire.

Il faut aussi prendre des bonnes chaussures de marche ou de tennis, à semelles plates. Dans les médines, les voitures, charrettes, gens et animaux circulent tous ensemble à une petite allure régulière sur les ruelles étroites, et il faut être prêt à s'écarter rapidement!

En décidant de votre tenue, soyez conscients de l'endroit où vous êtes. Dans les villages au bord de la mer ou autour des piscines des hôtels, des shorts courts et des habits étriqués sont acceptables, mais il est préférable de se couvrir un peu dans les villes et dans les régions rurales. Le Maroc est un pays musulman où les règles de convenance ne sont pas comme les nôtres. Bien que vous ne soyiez pas obligés de vous comporter comme des musulmans, cela vaut bien la peine de respecter leurs coutumes.

Average Temperatures

	January	*February*	*March*	*April*	*May*	*June*	*July*	*August*	*September*	*October*	*November*	*December*
Agadir	70	71	73	75	76	78	85	86	80	78	76	70
Al Hoceima	61	62	65	67	72	78	83	85	81	74	69	63
Casablanca	63	63	66	68	72	75	81	81	80	77	68	64
Essaouira	64	64	64	66	68	68	72	70	70	70	68	66
Fez	61	63	66	72	79	88	97	97	90	81	66	61
Marrakesh	70	71	73	79	84	86	92	97	88	82	75	70
Meknes	59	61	64	70	74	84	93	93	86	79	66	61
Ouarzazate	63	67	73	80	86	96	98	99	93	80	70	62
Rabat	63	64	66	70	73	77	82	82	81	77	68	64
Tangier	60	62	64	67	72	77	80	82	79	73	65	62
Taroudant	72	73	79	81	86	90	97	98	95	90	77	72
Safi	64	66	68	72	77	81	86	86	82	79	70	66
Zagora	69	73	75	80	85	90	97	98	92	86	78	70

Temperature Conversion Chart

°C	-30	-25	-20	-15	-10	-5	0	5	10	15	20	25	30	35	40	45

°F	-20	-10	0	10	20	30	40	50	60	70	80	90	100	110

ELEANOR HOFFMAN
The First Lady of Moroccan Rugs

I met Miss Hoffman in 1978 when I was giving a lecture on Morocco in Santa Barbara, California. She was 82 years old. Her first words to me were, "Young man, I need to sit close to you so I can hear," and "You said this Moroccan rug is about 40 years old. Come to my house and I will show you one that was 40 years old when I bought it in Morocco 40 years ago."

Miss Hoffman was elegant, with an Old World refinement which was new to me. Her blue eyes twinkled with excitement as she spoke. She told me she was a writer, born December 21st, 1895, in Belmont, Massachusetts. She had attended Radcliffe College and had lived in Santa Barbara for the past 40 years. Her father, Ralph Hoffman, had been the director of the Santa Barbara Museum of Natural History. Miss Hoffman had authored many children's books set in foreign countries, including *Mischief in Fez,* about the Sultan Moulay Ismail in the form of a mischievous boy. She also authored *Realm of the Evening Star-A History of Morocco and the Moors*. Miss Hoffman had searched Morocco for rugs and studied the country since the early 1940's. I was in awe, and love, and I had found my best friend.

In 1982, Eleanor and I packed our bags and headed for the Middle Atlas Mountains of Morocco. In a Berber home in Tiflet, she had her first opportunity to spend a night on a stack of rugs. As with everything, Eleanor found the experience "wonderful." In Rabat, she made her way up and down Avenue Mohammed V by herself, slowly, but with no problem. Eleanor said, "I just stand at the corners and the nice policemen help me across the streets." A man working at the Hotel Balima recognized her from forty years earlier. Taxi drivers asked her questions about Morocco. Her answers thrilled them. In Marrakesh, we attended the Folklore Festival together, where the Tuareg women in their flowing blue robes surrounded her, touching her so lovingly. A three-day case of bronchitis knocked her flat, but didn't dampen her spirits. The Hotel Marrakesh catered to her splendidly. Everyone in Morocco who met Eleanor felt rewarded. They always ask about her; the friends we made together five years later on Maui feel the same way.

Eleanor Hoffman passed away on December 20th, 1990, at her home in Santa Barbara, one day before her 95th birthday, still talking about her first love, Morocco.

Speaking for myself and the friends you touched across two oceans: Eleanor, you taught us the value of sweet words. We will always remember you.

ELEANOR HOFFMAN
La première dame des tapis marocains

J'avais rencontré Mlle. Hoffman pendant une conférence sur le Maroc que j'avais donnée en 1978 à Santa Barbara, Californie. Elle avait 82 ans. Les premières paroles qu'elle m'a adressées furent les suivantes: "Jeune homme, je dois m'asseoir plus près de vous pour pouvoir vous entendre," et aussi, "vous dites que ce tapis marocain date d'il y a 40 ans. Venez chez moi, et je vous montrerai un tapis qui avait déjà 40 ans quand je l'ai acheté au Maroc voilà 40 ans."

Mlle. Hoffman était élégante, avec un raffinement d'antan qui m'était tout nouveau. Ses yeux bleux étincelaient quand elle parlait. Elle me dit qu'elle était écrivaine, née le 21 décembre 1895 à Belmont, Massachussetts. Elle avait fait ses études à Radcliffe et habitait à Santa Barbara depuis 40 ans. Son père, Ralph Hoffman, avait été le directeur du Santa Barbara Museum of Natural History. Mlle. Hoffman avait écrit plusieurs livres d'enfants qui se déroulaient à l'étranger, y compris Mischief in Fez, *avec le sultan Moulay Ismail dans le rôle d'un petit coquin. Elle est aussi l'auteur du livre* Realm of the Evening Star - A History of Morocco and the Moors. *Mlle. Hoffman avait fouillé le Maroc à la recherche de tapis et avait étudié ce pays depuis le début des années 1940. Je fus épris d'admiration et d'amour pour cette dame, et j'avais trouvé ma meilleure amie.*

En 1982, Eleanor et moi fîmes nos valises et partîmes pour le Moyen Atlas du Maroc. Dans un foyer berbère à Tiflet, elle eu sa première occasion de passer la nuit sur une pile de tapis. Comme pour toutes ses aventures, Eleanor a trouvé cette expérience "merveilleuse." A Rabat, elle faisait toute seule son chemin le long de l'avenue Mohammed V, lentement mais sans problèmes. Elle me dit, "J'attends au coin et les gentils gendarmes m'aident à traverser la rue." Un homme qui travaillait à l'Hôtel Balima la reconnut après quarante ans. Les chauffeurs de taxi lui posaient des questions sur le Maroc, et ses réponses les émerveillaient. Nous assistâmes ensemble au Festival d'Arts folkoriques à Marrakech, où les femmes touarègues, dans leurs robes bleues flottantes, l'entourèrent en l'embrassant très affectueusement.

Une bronchite de trois jours l'anéantit pendant un moment, mais ne la découragea pas. Tout le monde qui la rencontrait au Maroc se sentait heureux de faire sa connaissance, et on demande toujours de ces nouvelles; c'est de même pour les amis que nous fîmes 5 ans plus tard à Maui, Hawaii.

Eleanor Hoffman est morte le 20 décembre, 1990, dans sa maison à Santa Barbara, un jour avant son 95ème anniversaire...et parlant toujours de son premier amour, le Maroc.

De ma part et de celle des amis que vous avez touchés à travers deux océans, je voudrais vous dire, Eleanor, que vous nous avez appris la valeur des mots doux. Nous nous rappellerons toujours de vous.

Photo: J. Taylor

Lahsan, A rug trimmer of Marrakesh with the author.
Lahsan, un garnisseur de tapis de Marrakech avec l'auteur.

The Language of the Heart

If you have a rug that needs trimming, Lahsan is the best man to take it to in Marrakesh. Unless you speak Arabic, you may want to bring an interpreter along, but it's all right if you don't, because Lahsan, like so many Moroccans, speaks only Arabic and what I call "the language of the heart." He smiles, laughs, waves his arms, and gestures animatedly. He realizes that you are as lost as he is, and makes the best of it by keeping things light and easy. . . and your rug will surely turn out beautifully.

Any attempt that you make to speak Arabic in Morocco will be met with delight and encouragement. Here are a few useful words and phrases to start you off. . .

Le language du coeur

Si vous avez un tapis dont les bords ont besoin d'être rognés, la meilleure personne pour le faire à Marrakech, c'est Lahsan. Si vous ne parlez pas l'arabe, un interprète vous serait utile, mais si vous n'en amenez pas ça ne fait rien, parce que Lahsan, comme beaucoup d'autres Marocains, ne parle que l'arabe et ce que j'appelle "le language du coeur." Il sourit, il rit, il gesticule avec animation. Il se rend compte que vous êtes aussi perdus que lui, et il s'en accommode en maintenant une atmosphère joyeuse et décontractée...et votre tapis est sûr d'être fini à merveille.

Toute tentative que vous faites de parler l'arabe au Maroc sera accueillie avec grand plaisir et beaucoup d'encouragement. Voici quelques mots et phrases utiles pour commencer:

Hello	*bonjour*	ahlan
Goodbye	*aurevoir*	beslama
Excuse me	*pardon*	smahlia
I understand	*je comprends*	fham't
I don't understand	*je ne comprends pas*	ma fham tsh
Thank you	*merci*	shoukran
How are you?	*comment allez-vous?*	labass alaik
Sure, why not	*D'accord, pourquoi pas*	allash la
Very good	très bien	mazian
Please	s'il vous plaît	shoukran
Help me please	*pourriez-vous m'aider?*	aounni affak
Doctor	*docteur*	tabib
Bread	*pain*	khoubz
Butter	*beurre*	zabda
How much?	*combien?*	bsh-hal
The grace	*la prière*	shahada
Divine protection	*protection divine*	el baraka
Holy man	*saint homme*	shaikh
There is no problem	*pas de problème*	ma kainsh moushkil
Money	*argent*	flouss
Hotel	*hôtel*	fundak
Mecca	*la Mecque*	Mecca
Antique	*antique*	qadim
All of it	*tout*	koulshi
Food	*nourriture*	makla
Coffee	*café*	qahwa
Milk	*lait*	halib
Orange juice	*jus d'orange*	assir limoun
Much	*beaucoup*	bizaf
Little	*peu*	saghir
I have no money	*je n'ai pas d'argent*	ma andish flouss
Laundry	*lessive*	tasbin
Maid	*femme de chambre*	khadama
Tailor	*tailleur*	khaiat
Left	*à gauche*	lissar
Right	*à droite*	liman
Up	*en haut*	fug
Down	*en bas*	taht
Good	*bien*	mazian
Bad	*mauvais*	khaieb
Hot	*chaud*	skhoun
Cold	*froid*	bared
Cheap	*bon marché*	rakhiss
Expensive	*cher*	ghalli
Old	*vieux*	qadim
New	*nouveau*	jadid
Move aside	*écartez-vous*	ballak

Photo: Author

Hadj Ahmed Sarmi Ben Rahal, Marrakesh.
Hadj Ahmed Sarmi Ben Rahal, Marrakech.

Photo: Author

Hadj Alouani Bibi Mehdi and wife, Marrakesh.
Hadj Alouani Bibi Mehdi et son épouse, Marrakech.

THE HADJ
In Memoriam

"Hadj" is a title given to Moslem men upon completing their pilgrimage to the Holy City of Mecca, in Saudi Arabia. The women are called "Hadja." This is a title of earned respect, often designated by the man wearing a golden colored turban.

This book is in loving memory of Hadj Sarmi Ben Rahal and Hadj Alouani Bibi Mehdi, of Marrakesh, who opened their hearts and homes to me, and spent so much time in their final years teaching me the rug business.

LE HADJ
In Memoriam

"Hadj" est un titre donné aux hommes muslumans quand ils ont complété leur pèlerinage à la sainte ville de la Mecque, en Arabie Saoudite. Les femmes s'appellent "Hadja." C'est un titre de respect gagné par leurs efforts, et les hommes qui le possèdent sont désignés par un turban de couleur dorée.

Ce livre est dédié à la mémoire de Hadj Sarmi Ben Rahal et de Hadj Alouani Bibi Mehdi, de Marrakech, qui m'ont ouvert leurs coeurs et leurs maisons, et qui ont passé tant de temps pendant leurs dernières années à m'apprendre le commerce des tapis.

Acknowledgements

I would like to mention some of the people who are responsible for *A Treasure Hunter's Guide to Morocco*. I'll begin with those responsible for making "Treasures" understandable for us all, my photographers: Randall Hahn, of Prints Unlimited in Dallas, Texas, spent two weeks in Morocco with my Western Artists tour, at which time he took three thousand pictures! My friend Stephen Hampton, a New York fashion photographer, has accompanied me to Morocco on numerous occasions. Steve Grant from Des Moines, Iowa, photographed the embroidery on page 109. Gary Gingrich from Kansas City photographed the book cover and the Bronze Horseman. Balf Walker from Tucson, Arizona, went into the Middle Atlas Mountains with me and took a lot of great tribal shots. Gavin Sisk from Seattle, Washington, is my contemplative photographer. Watch for Gavin's on-location photography in *The Doors of the Moors*. Bertrand of Marrakesh has an extensive library of slides for tourists, and I would like to express my special gratitude to Mr. Linh of Morocco for his magnificent photograph of His Majesty King Hassan.

The "Treasure Map" on page 3 was created by Vivian Mungall, a calligrapher for Zillers of Kansas City, and by Tucson airbrush artist Bill Boyer. Judi Taylor and David Arnold assisted me in my research. I'd like to thank Mrs. Ruth Rotert for organizing my typing and helping with the editing of "Treasures." Wendy Voorhees in Tucson did a fine job setting the type, and Rod Hanes at American Color in Tucson made the color separations. I also owe special thanks to Dr. Tad Park of the University of Arizona, Dr. Rohn Eloul and Isabelle Houthakker of Intercultural Enterprises, Tucson, for the French translation and final editing.

I'd like to thank Mustapha Alaoui of Rabat for his help in Morocco, and his sons Omar and Hassan Alaoui for their help with the Arabic translations.

All of these technical components were put into the hands of John Davis, Sandra Dixon and the competent staff of Arizona Lithographers in Tucson, Arizona, who turned them into the book you're holding.

My museum colleagues are: Claire Campbell Park, curator of "Resplendent Diversity" and co-author of *From the Far West: Carpets and Textiles of Morocco*, edited by Patricia L. Fiske, W. Russell Pickering and Ralph S. Yohe (available through the Textile Museum in Washington, D.C.). Mrs. Park is a fiber artist, an independent museum curator and an art professor at Pima Community College in Tucson. I'd also like to thank Old Pueblo Museum Director Dr. Christene Conti and Installation Director Rick Busselle, who were responsible for the "Resplendent Diversity" exhibit.

Lynn Denton, who wrote the chapter on embroidery, is the Assistant Director of the Texas Memorial Museum in Austin, Texas. Mrs. Denton worked with the Moroccan museums to coordinate the 1987 Commemorative Morocco-U.S. Treaty Exhibition at the Texas Memorial Museum.

Dee Bryers, author of "Artists of the American West in Morocco," lives in Sonoita, Arizona.

Ms. Jerry Whitney's feelings about Morocco are revealed in her article "Tribal Capes and Ceremonial Blankets."

I'd like to thank Ambassador Michael Ussery in Rabat and Ambassador Mohamed Belkhayat in Washington, D.C. for their contributions, Mrs. Matilda Revah at the Moroccan Embassy in Washington, D.C. for her assistance, Mr. John Bircher and Miss Jennifer Notkin of Neill and Company in Washington, D.C. and A. Salah Eddine Tazi for their time, consideration and liaison assistance.

I'd also like to think my good friend in Kansas City, Harry McLear, for his contribution and lessons in diplomacy.

To properly thank all of the people who have made this book possible would require a book in itself. . . From the first Moroccan family who shared their couscous with me, to each client who ever bought one of my rugs, I thank you all from the bottom of my heart.

Alf Taylor

Remerciements

Je voudrais mentionner quelques-unes des personnes responsables du Guide du Maroc pour les chasseurs de trésors. *D'abord, ceux qui ont illustré mon livre, les photographes: Randall Hahn des Prints Unlimited à Dallas, Texas, a passé deux semaines au Maroc avec mon tour d'Artistes de l'Ouest, et a pris trois mille photos pendant le voyage! Mon ami Stephen Hampton, un photographe de mode de New York, m'a accompagné au Maroc à plusieurs occasions. Steve Grant de Des Moines, Iowa, a photographié la broderie à la page 109. Gary Gingrich de Kansas City a photographié la couverture du livre et le cavalier de bronze. Balf Walker de Tucson, Arizona, est venu avec moi au Moyen Atlas et a pris beaucoup de belles photos tribales. Gavin Sisk de Seattle, Washington, est mon photographe contemplatif. Vous verrez les photos en extérieur de Gavin dans les* Portes des Maures. *Bertrand de Marrakech possède une vaste bilbiothèque de diapositives pour les touristes; et je voudrais exprimer ma gratitude particulière à M. Linh du Maroc de sa magnifique photo de Sa Majesté le Roi Hassan.*

La "Carte de trésors" à la page 3 est la création de Vivian Muncall, une artiste calligraphique chez Zillers de Kansas City, et de l'artiste du pinceau à l'air Bill Boyer, de Tucson. Judi Taylor et David Arnold m'ont assisté dans ma recherche. Je voudrais aussi remercier Madame Ruth Rotert d'avoir organizé ma dactylographie et de m'avoir aidé à éditer les "trésors." Wendy Voorhees à Tucson a fait la composition excellente, et Rod Hanes de l'American Color à Tucson a fait les séparations des couleurs. Je voudrais aussi exprimer ma reconnaissance particulière envers le Dr. Tad Park de l'Université d'Arizona, le Dr. Rohn Eloul et Isabelle Houthakker d'Intercultural Enterprises, à Tucson, d'avoir traduit ce livre en français et de son édition finale.

Je suis très reconnaissant à Mustapha Alaoui de Rabat de son aide au Maroc, et à ses fils Omar et Hassan Alaoui de leur aide avec la traduction en arabe.

John Davis, Sandra Dixon et le personnel compétent d'Arizona Lithographers à Tucson, Arizona, on pris en charge toutes ces composantes techniques, et les ont transformées en ce livre que vous tenez dans vos mains.

Mes collègues de musée sont les suivants: Claire Campbell Park, la conservatrice de la "Diversité resplendissante" et coauteur du livre De l'extrême occident: tapis et textiles du Maroc, *édité par Patricia L. Fiske, W. Russell Pickering et Ralph S. Yohe (distribué par le Textile Museum à Washington, D.C.). Mme. Park est une artiste de textiles, une conservatrice de musée indépendante, et professeur d'art au Pima Community College à Tucson. Je voudrais aussi remercier le directeur de l'Old Pueblo Museum, le Dr. Christine Conti, et le directeur d'installation, Rick Busselle, qui étaient responsables de l'exhibition de "Diversité resplendissante."*

Lynn Denton, qui a écrit le chapitre sur la broderie, est la directrice adjointe du Texas Memorial Museum à Austin, Texas. Mme. Denton a travaillé avec les musées marocains pour coordonner en 1987 l'Exhibition commémorative du Traité entre les Etats-Unis et le Maroc au Texas Memorial Museum.

Dee Bryers, l'auteur des "Artistes de l'Ouest américain au Maroc" habite à Sonoita, Arizona.

Me. Jerry Whitney exprime ses sentiments à l'égard du Maroc dans son article "Capes et couvertures cérémonielles tribales."

Je voudrais exprimer ma gratitude envers Monsieur l'Ambassadeur Michael Ussery à Rabat et Monsieur l'Ambassadeur Mohammed Belkhayat à Washington de leurs contributions, envers Mme. Matilda Revah à l'Ambassade du Maroc à Washington, D.C. de son assistance, et envers M. John Bircher et Mlle. Jennifer Notkin de Neill and Company à Washington, D.C. et A. Salah Eddine Tazi de leur temps, efforts et assistance de liaison.

Je voudrais aussi remercier mon cher ami Harry McLear de Kansas City de ses contributions et de ses leçons de diplomatie.

Il me faudrait tout un livre pour remercier convenablement tous ceux qui ont rendu ce livre possible...depuis la première famille marocaine qui ait partagé son couscous avec moi jusqu'à tous mes clients qui aient jamais acheté un de mes tapis, je vous remercie tous du fond de mon coeur.

Alf Taylor

Photo: J. Taylor

Alf Taylor and Harry McLear, Honorary Consul of Morocco.
Alf Taylor et Harry McLear, Consul honoraire du Maroc.

Morocco with the Author

by Harry McLear
Honorary Consul of the Kingdom of Morocco

We are told as children that our dreams will come true, and for me that dream did become a reality with my first visit to Morocco. As a young man, I was always intrigued by this most fascinating Arab country on a faraway continent, recalling my history lessons which told me that Morocco has been a friend of the United States since the time of George Washington. This tie of friendship was clearly demonstrated to me by officials and merchants, but most of all by the people.

As Honorary Consul of Morocco, I had my first visit to this enthralling land last March at the invitation of His Majesty King Hassan II, to attend the Fête du Trône. This annual event honors the accession of King Hassan II to the throne. As I watched and listened, I discovered that in a sense it was really a celebration of the people. The costumes, the music and the adulation expressed for the King made it a very moving experience. The motto of Morocco is "God, the Nation, the King." After having attended the Fête, and after having had the opportunity to reflect, I believe that it truly describes the mystique of this beautiful country.

With time to travel and shop, I chose my friend, Alf Taylor, the author of this book, to escort me literally into the inner sanctums of Morocco. As an American, his knowledge of Morocco and fellowship with the Moroccan people were most impressive. As a representative of the Moroccan government in the United States, I wanted very much to meet and see the people as they work and live. With Alf Taylor this was made possible. From the souks and snake charmers to the ancient imperial palaces, I saw Morocco as one should see it: a friendly, deeply religious country steeped in history, treasures and good will toward all. It was like my childhood dream—beautiful, mysterious, intriguing and romantic. Mr. Taylor once told me, "God, I love this country..." and the sparkle in his eyes when we talk about Morocco says it again and again.

September 28, 1990

Au Maroc avec l'auteur

par Harry McLear
Consul honoraire du Royaume du Maroc

Quand nous sommes petits on nous dit que nos rêves vont se réaliser, et pour moi, mon rêve c'est réalisé avec ma première visite au Maroc. Quand j'étais jeune, j'étais toujours intrigué par ce pays arabe si fascinant dans un continent lointain, en me souvenant de mes leçons d'histoire qui m'avaient appris que le Maroc avait été ami avec les Etats-Unis depuis le temps de George Washington. Les fonctionnaires et marchants, et surtout le peuple, m'ont démontré clairement ce lien d'amitié.

En tant que Consul honoraire du Maroc, j'ai visité pour la première fois ce pays passionnant à l'invitation de Sa Majesté le Roi Hassan II, pour assister à la fête du Trône en mars de cette année. Cet événement annuel fait honneur à l'accession au trône du Roi Hassan II. Tout en regardant et en écoutant, j'ai découvert que dans un sens c'était vraiment une célébration du peuple. Les costumes, la musique et l'adulation exprimée pour le Roi en ont fait une expérience très émouvante. La devise du Maroc est "Dieu, la Nation, le Roi." Après avoir assisté à la fête et après avoir eu l'occasion de réfléchir à ce sujet, je constate que ceci décrit réellement la mystique de ce beau pays.

Comme j'avais du temps pour voyager et faire des achats, j'ai choisi mon ami Alf Taylor, l'auteur de ce livre, pour me faire entrer litéralement dans les sanctuaires du Maroc. En tant qu'Américain, ses connaissances du Maroc et son amitié avec le peuple marocain sont très impressionnantes. Comme représentant du gouvernement du Maroc aux Etats-Unis, je voulais beaucoup rencontrer et voir les gens à leur travail et vie ordinaires. Ceci devint possible avec Alf Taylor. Des souks et charmeurs de serpents jusqu'aux anciens palais impériaux, j'ai vu le Maroc comme il faut le voir: un pays amical et profondément religieux imprégné d'histoire, de trésors et de bonne volonté envers tous. C'était comme mon rêve d'enfance—beau, mystérieux, intrigant et romantique. M. Taylor m'a dit une fois, "Mon Dieu, ce que j'aime ce pays..." et l'étincelle qui brille dans ses yeux quand nous parlons du Maroc reflète ce sentiment maintes et maintes fois.

28 septembre 1990

Photos: Author/Sisk

Koutoubia Mosque, Marrakesh: Antique window, AMMA.
Mosquée de Koutoubia, Marrakech: ancienne fenêtre, AMMA.